MASTERING AUTO-TUNE

MASTERING AUTO-TUNE

Max Mobley

Hal Leonard Books
An Imprint of Hal Leonard Corporation

Published in 2013 by Hal Leonard Books
An Imprint of Hal Leonard Corporation
7777 West Bluemound Road
Milwaukee, WI 53213

Trade Book Division Editorial Offices
33 Plymouth St., Montclair, NJ 07042

Photo of the Gregory Brothers (epigraph figure and figure 1.3) by Denny Renshaw

Printed in the United States of America

Book design by Adam Fulrath
Book composition by Kristina Rolander

Library of Congress Cataloging-in-Publication Data

Mobley, Max.
 Mastering Auto-tune / Max Mobley.
     p. cm.
 Includes bibliographical references and index.
 1. Auto-tune (Computer file) 2. Computer sound processing. I. Title.
 ML74.4.A87M63 2013
 781.49'028553–dc23
                                          2012039989

ISBN 978-1-4768-1417-9

www.halleonardbooks.com

Figure E.1. The Gregory Brothers (Michael, Andrew, Evan, and Sarah) are best known for their popular "Auto-Tune the News" series of music videos. As of mid-2012, "Bed Intruder Song" from the series had been viewed over 101 million times! YouTube listed the song as the most popular video of 2010.

People often ask us: Why "Auto-Tune the News?" Well, it's simple really. There's no other computer program in the world that works automatically quite like Auto-Tune. To tune something by hand, as Bach once tuned his clavicle or whatever it's called, would take forever and also be the gloomiest of drudgeries. So when we found out about Auto-Tune, a program that would automatically do absolutely all of our work for us, we promptly spent years inventing fiber-optics, creating the World Wide Web, and patenting, trademarking, copywriting, and reserving the rights to anything having to do with the catch-phrase of the decade: "social media content creator." It just rolls off the tongue, doesn't it? By simply applying it to the speaking voices of folks to make them sing, we were finally able to lazily and automatically use Auto-Tune to do all of our work for us. Never in the history of the world has anyone made 50 billion dollars quicker!

—The Gregory Brothers

CONTENTS

Acknowledgments xiii

Chapter 1

An Auto-Tune Primer 1
Powerful Tool or Overused Effect (or Both)?....................................... 1
What Auto-Tune Does.. 2
What Auto-Tune Does Not Do.. 3
Audio Sources Suitable for Auto-Tune.. 3
Which Version of Auto-Tune Do I Need? 4
    Auto-Tune EFX 2... 6
    Auto-Tune Live 6
    Auto-Tune Evo and Auto-Tune Version 7....................................... 7

Chapter 2

Adding Auto-Tune to Your Studio..9
A Bit About Bits 9
    Auto-Tune Installation on 32-Bit and 64-Bit Machines 9
    64-Bit Apple Logic Pro and Auto-Tune.. 10
    Apple's Mountain Lion Gatekeeper.. 10
Mysteries of the iLok Revealed.. 11
    Authorizing Auto-Tune via the iLok System................................... 11
Auto-Tune Plug-in Formats 12
    Plug-in Format Types 12
    DAW Plug-in Format Compatibility List....................................... 12
Optimizing Your DAW for Auto-Tune... 13
    Safe and Easy System Optimization Steps..................................... 13
Managing Multiple Instances of Auto-Tune in Large Projects 14
    Auto-Tune in the Signal Path.. 15
    Auto-Tune and TDM... 15
Optimizing Auto-Tune for your DAW... 16
    Options Dialog: Buffer Size... 16
    Options Dialog: Undo.. 17
    Options Dialog: Default Retune Speed 17
    Options Dialog: Key Bindings.. 17
    Save Options as Default... 17
    Data File Management.. 17

Chapter 3

The Correction Modes:
Automatic (Auto) Mode Versus Graphical (Graph) Mode 19

Picking the Right Correction Mode...20
    Auto Mode Has Two Distinct Advantages over
        Graphical Mode...20
    Try Auto Mode When 20
    Graphical Mode Has Two Distinct Advantages over
        Auto Mode...21
    Try Graphical Mode When 21
Trade-Offs Between Auto Mode and Graphical Mode 21
Auto Mode and Real Time Pitch Correction 21
Auto Mode and Graphical Mode Working Together 22

Chapter 4

Mastering Pitch Correction in Automatic Mode......................... 23

A Tour of Auto Mode's Controls 23
    Input Type..23
    Tracking..24
    Key and Scale 24
    Target Notes..25
    Scale Detune..25
    Using Scale Detune to Determine Your Song's
        Reference Pitch 25
    Transpose 25
    Formant...25
    Throat Length 25
    Pitch Change Amount Indicator 26
    Edit Scale Display 26
Virtual Keyboard, Keyboard Edit, and Keyboard Mode..................27
    Latch Mode and Momentary Mode 28
The Pitch Correction Control Section...28
    A Tour of the Pitch Control Section Parameters 28
Using Auto Mode for Transparent, Professional Pitch Correction ... 29
    It's All About Retune Speed..29
    Humanizing Pitch Correction 29
    Keeping Natural Vibrato Natural 30
The Create Vibrato Section..30
    A Tour of the Create Vibrato Section Controls 30
MIDI and Auto Mode 31
    A Tour of the Auto Mode MIDI Controls 31

Chapter 5

The Power of Graphical Mode..**33**
  Graphical Mode Housekeeping...34
    Clock Source and Clock Display.......................................34
    Buffer Size..35
    Default Retune Speed 36
  Life Inside the Pitch Graph Display 37
    The Time and Pitch Axes...37
    Time Display..38
    Pitch Reference Lines and Lanes 38
    Auto Scroll..38
    Envelope Graph Display..39
    All/Tie 39
    Parameters Shared Between Auto Mode and Graphical Mode 39
  Tracking Audio for Pitch Correction 40
    Track Pitch..40
  Graphical Mode Correction Objects 42
    Red Curves, Blue Curves, Green Curves...........................42
    Creating Blue Curve Correction Objects...........................44
    Line Correction Objects...45
    Note Correction Objects..45
    The Mighty Make Notes Button 45
    Number of Note Objects Knob...46
    Nudging Objects...46
  Graphical Mode Tools in Detail...46
    Correction Object Drawing Tools.....................................47
    Navigation and Object Editing Tools 47
  Graphical Mode Edit Buttons 49
    Selecting Correction Objects for Editing...........................50
  Graphical Mode as a Pitch Analyzer 50
    Object Pitch Display..50
    Output Pitch Display...50
    Detected Pitch Display...50
    Cursor Time Position Display 51

Chapter 6

Mastering Pitch Correction in Graphical Mode **53**
  Correcting with Curves...53
    Correction Curves with a Single Click 53
    Using the Make Curve Button 55
    The Art of Drawing Curves 56
    Reasons for Breaking out the Curve Tool..........................57

Correcting with Lines 60
    Drawing Correction Object Lines 60
    Editing and Moving Line Objects with the Arrow Tool.............. 65
    Adding or Removing Anchor Points.................................... 65
    Experimenting with Per-Object Parameters 66
    Per-Object Retune Speed... 66
    Per-Object Adjust Vibrato.. 67
    Per-Object Throat Length Adjust....................................... 67
    Line Object Segments and Per-Object Parameters 68
    The Scissor Tool and Per-Object Parameters 68
Correcting Notes with Notes 69
    Making Notes with a Single Click....................................... 69
    Number of Note Objects.. 70
Mixing Correction Objects.. 70
    Correction Object Roundup... 71
Using Auto Mode and Graphical Mode Together............................ 71
    Importable Auto Mode Parameters 73

Chapter 7

Auto-Tune Live **75**
Auto-Tune Live = Auto Mode 76
Real-Time MIDI Control... 76
    Auto-Tune Live's Real-Time MIDI Controls 76
    OMNI and MIDI Channels.. 76
Using Auto-Tune Live Onstage... 77
    Setting up a MIDI Controller and Auto-Tune Live 77
MIDI Assignable Parameters in Auto-Tune Live............................ 78

Chapter 8

Creating Vibrato with Auto-Tune **79**
Creating Vibrato After Tracking 79
    Vibrato Research.. 80
Vibrato and the Auto-Tune Effect 80
Creating Natural-Sounding Vibrato in Auto Mode 81
    Vibrato Shape 81
    Pitch, Amplitude, and Formant Amounts 81
    Vibrato Rate 81
    Variation 81
    Onset Delay and Onset Rate 81
Vibrato Automation... 82
Vibrato Management 82
    When to Use Targeting Ignores Vibrato.............................. 83

Vibrato Control in Graphical Mode 83
   Adjust Vibrato in Action 83
   Dialing In Vibrato in Graphical Mode 84
   Creating Vibrato in Graphical Mode 85

Chapter 9

MIDI and Auto-Tune **87**
MIDI and Auto Mode 87
   Learn Scale From MIDI 88
   Using Learn Scale From MIDI 88
   Using Target Notes Via MIDI 90
   MIDI and Octave Mode 90
   Turn off MIDI Features When Done 90
Working with MIDI and Graphical Mode 91
   Keep It Monophonic 91
   Tracking Audio with MIDI 91
   Make Notes From MIDI 91
   MIDI in the Pitch Graph Display 92

Chapter 10

Mastering the Auto-Tune Vocal Effect **93**
Using Auto Mode to Create the Auto-Tune Effect 93
   The Power of Retune Speed 93
   The Wrong Key Opens the Right Door 94
   Transpose Down, Then Tune Up 94
   Transpose with Discretion 95
   A Scalable Solution 96
Mastering the Auto-Tune Effect in Graphical Mode 96
   Using Note Objects for Melody and the Auto-Tune Effect 96
MIDI and the Auto-Tune Effect 98

Chapter 11

Auto-Tune on Musical Instruments **101**
Monophonic Matters 101
Setting up Auto-Tune for Musical Instruments 101
   Input Type 102
   Retune Speed for Instruments 102
   Keep It Real 102
Detune with Auto-Tune 103
Experiments with Pitch 103

Chapter 12

Auto-Tune Time Compression and Expansion **105**

Tracking Pitch and Time 106
The Time Control Section 106
  Enable (Time) 107
  Undo (Time) 107
  Redo (Time) 107
  Clear All (Time) 107
Auto-Tune's Time Tools 107
  The Move Point Tool 108
  The Move Region Tool 110
Time Preserves Pitch 112
Picking the Right Time Tool 112
The Data Error Indicator 113

Appendix: About the DVD-ROM **115**
Index **117**

ACKNOWLEDGMENTS

Thanks to the Gregory Brothers, Grego Ondo and Steinberg, Derk Hagedorn, Anders Steele, and Bill Gibson at Hal Leonard, Inc. In-and-out-of-tune vocals provided by Tina Davy; music provided by Bobby One-Sock Templin. Additional music provided by The Cranks of Santa Cruz, CA, with vocal by Mike Hilden.

MASTERING AUTO-TUNE

Chapter 1
AN AUTO-TUNE PRIMER

Auto-Tune has become an indispensable pro audio tool for all levels of audio production. Whether you are aiming for the popular vocal effect or pitch correction so discrete no one knows it has been applied, this book will help you master the technology and incorporate it into your music.

Powerful Tool or Overused Effect (or Both)?

Among music fans, the term *Auto-Tune* has become synonymous with a certain heavily processed vocal effect popular in modern music. Think of Cher's hit "Believe," or most of hip hop artist T-Pain's body of work, or the Black Eyed Peas hit "I Gotta Believe," which was played at 2011's Super Bowl halftime show. Across many genres of popular music, the Auto-Tune effect has become ubiquitous, so much so that it has become a cultural meme.

Figure 1.1

Among audio engineers, music producers, and music makers, Auto-Tune is better known as an indispensable tool for correcting vocal performances that stray too far flat or sharp. When it is used as a pitch correction tool, listeners are not even aware that Auto-Tune has been applied to the song they are hearing. In fact, if you own any popular Western music with vocals produced after 1997, then most likely Auto-Tune lives in your music library much the way Pro Tools software and Gibson and Fender guitars live in your music library. This is not a bad thing. The truth is, pitch correction has become as important to music production as reverb and EQ.

Randy Jackson, the Grammy award–winning judge on the popular singing show American Idol, often tells contestants who have turned in an off-key performance that they are pitchy, dawg! That is exactly what Auto-Tune is designed to address. In fact, one could argue that the pervasive use of Auto-Tune in popular music as a pitch correction tool and not as an effect has trained our ears to know when a singer is "pitchy." Imperfections are, however, common and arguably essential to art. Frank Sinatra, Elvis Presley, Janis Joplin, Al Green—all have, by today's standards, more

Figure 1.2

than one pitchy moment in their recorded bodies of work. The fact that we are now aware of this can largely be attributed to the ubiquitous use of Auto-Tune. And this brings up a very important point—perfection and imperfection both have their places in music. Knowing when to stop is just as important as knowing where to begin.

What Auto-Tune Does

Auto-Tune lives solely in the digital domain. When used in real time, it works directly on the audio waveforms it is processing, constantly monitoring the frequencies (pitches) of the waveform being processed, and then modifying this data on the fly in order to move it to the desired note. And it does this with remarkable speed and precision. Keep in mind that in regard to this book and Auto-Tune, the terms pitch, note, and frequency are largely interchangeable.

The above definition of how pitch correction works is oversimplified, and of course, what is really going on is serious amounts of math, optimized to operate in real time, without introducing any artifacts or transients to the media being processed. If you have ever tried to create a loop of an audio sample that is fairly constant—like that of a violin sample, for instance—you know how hard it can be to make those loop points sound seamless. That should give some idea of the power behind the Auto-Tune algorithm.

As you incorporate pitch correction into your music production work, you will find that even the best vocalists will have some unintentional variances in pitch. In other words, we are all, at various times, pitchy, dawg. Your job as an artist, engineer, or producer will be to tell Auto-Tune how long (time) and how far (pitch) a vocal performance can stray from the intended note before applying correction, and how precise that pitch correction should be. Master that, and you have mastered transparent pitch correction as found on all those songs that sound simply in tune, not "Auto-Tuned."

Of course, it takes more than just frequency manipulation for pitch correction to be transparent on vocal tracks, which it should unless the artist or producer is going for a vocal effect. The formant of the human vocal tract, along with well-honed vocal technique, is what makes a singer sound not only human but like him- or herself. It is why Celine Dion does not sound like Christina Aguilera and vice versa when they are singing the same song in the same key. These are things Auto-Tune takes into account and preserves, while at the same time serving them up as adjustable parameters available to the user.

Another key component to the natural sound of singing lies in how vocalists reach notes, and move from one note to another. People are not pianos, and when we sing, we do not jump from note to note like a piano. Instead, we glide, growl, and emote our way through the notes found in our melodies. Even in rock 'n' roll and rhythm and blues, where vocal melodies are often sung staccato and played out rapidly, there are important moments in the vocal performance where the singer is, however briefly, "in between notes." If Auto-Tune did not respect these and other natural elements of singing—and what's more, give its users control over them—then pitch correction would never, ever sound natural and transparent. One of the key parameters Auto-Tune offers up in this regard is Retune Speed, and it is something you will come to know well as you master Auto-Tune for your recordings. Retune Speed controls how quickly pitch correction is applied to material detected as out of tune. On Cher's 1998 hit single "Believe," producer Mark Taylor turned the Retune Speed knob to 0, and in doing so, introduced to the world what became known as "the Cher effect," and has since been dubbed "the T-Pain effect" (though T-Pain has now partnered with Izotope for his own brand of pitch correction), or simply Auto-Tune. Many music fans, musicians, and audio engineers from all over the world will remember the first time they heard that sound—and the subsequent debates over how it was created, since Taylor and his audio engineer kept quiet about how they did it, and at the time, few knew Auto-Tune could work in such a way.

What Auto-Tune Does Not Do

A popular misconception about Auto-Tune is that it allows people who cannot carry a tune in a bucket to become great singers with the push of a button. This is simply not true. Auto-Tune is not a substitute for talent, or practice and dedication to the craft of singing. In spite of heavy-handed use of the technology, T-Pain, Black Eyed Peas, and, of course, Cher all knew how to sing before Auto-Tune was ever applied to their voices. But what Auto-Tune has done for them and many others is to extend vocal ranges to some degree, fix a few bad notes in an otherwise great performance, make it easier to sound perfectly in tune, and perform with an iconic vocal effect. Because of this, Auto-Tune can save valuable time (and therefore money) in the studio by simplifying the audio production process.

It is usually around this part of the debate that someone brings up the very talented Gregory Brothers and their "Auto-Tune the News" songs and videos, heard and seen by millions via iTunes and YouTube. Keep in mind that those catchy numbers, including "Bed Intruder Song" and "Double Rainbow Song"—two songs that started as remixes lampooning quirky viral videos before turning into bona fide pop hits—employ (among other effects and techniques) the heavy use of Auto-Tune as both a melody creator and vocal effect. If you listen to both of the above-mentioned songs, the vocal sounds in each are very similar. This is, of course, intentional. It is also a byproduct of using a technology like Auto-Tune to create music from material that was not musical to begin with. If you're unfamiliar with the Gregory Brothers' work, you would do well to check them out. Their music is an excellent example of the power of Auto-Tune in the hands of some very creative individuals.

Figure 1.3

Along with mastering pitch correction for your vocal tracks, this book will show you how you can adapt these popular techniques for affecting vocals and modifying melodies as found in the works of T-Pain, Kanye West, and, yes, the Gregory Brothers.

And unless you are content with sounding 80 percent mechanical and 20 percent human, Auto-Tune is not a replacement for talent.

The vocal effect created with Auto-Tune as discussed in this book has been given many different names within the recording industry and music culture. For the sake of clarity, this book refers to that effect simply (and most accurately) as "the Auto-Tune effect."

Audio Sources Suitable for Auto-Tune

Auto-Tune only works with monophonic audio files (monophonic = one note at a time). Therefore, audio tracks or files that contain chords or multiple voices, such as a choir or group of background singers, are not suitable for Auto-Tune processing. The human voice is monophonic, making it ideal for pitch correction via Auto-Tune.

In addition, recording engineers and producers continue to find instances in which they need to apply pitch correction to non-vocal audio parts. In short, any recording of a monophonic instrument (or an instrument playing a monophonic part) that suffers from pitch and tuning problems can benefit from some amount of pitch correction. Discretion is advised, however, and any engineer will tell you that a balance between preserving the characteristics of the instrument and the need for perfect pitch should be respected. Nonetheless, from tin whistles in Irish folk music to Motown-inspired bass lines, Auto-Tune can help salvage off-key monophonic instrument performances.

Here are a few examples of instruments that can sometimes benefit from pitch correction via Auto-Tune:

- Folk Instruments: Folk and ethnic instruments often lack the means to meet the modern definition of what it means to be in tune, and this can be quite noticeable when they are used on songs that also contain modern instrumentation.
- Fretless Stringed Instruments: Fretless instruments such as violin, viola and cello require a high degree of skill in order to play them perfectly in tune. As long as the part is monophonic, fretless instrument parts can often benefit from Auto-Tune processing.
- Electric Bass: In most forms of pop and rock 'n' roll music, bass parts are usually single-line, monophonic parts. Applying Auto-Tune pitch correction to fretless bass lines is a no-brainer, but even fretted basses can sometimes benefit from the technology.
- Guitar Solos: Use of Auto-Tune on guitar solos that contain clearly defined single notes has become more common in recent years, but it is an area where the process must be used with surgical precision. Like other stringed instruments, guitars do not have perfect intonation (the instrument being in tune with itself), which therefore lends itself to pitch correction. Keep in mind that many people consider the guitar's lack of perfect intonation, and therefore its lack of perfect pitch, an integral part of its sound. Some of the most highly regarded electric guitars ever built lack the means to be intonated, or offer very limited intonation adjustment. Indeed, if you applied pitch correction to a solo by legendary blues guitar player B. B. King, you would be removing elements that help define King's style and signature sound. Any engineer using pitch correction, regardless of the instrument or the performance, needs to know not only when and how to use it, but when not to use it at all—art was never meant to be perfect.

Auto-Tune is a second-level solution. Pitch or tuning problems should be identified and addressed during the recording phase of the session whenever possible. Nothing beats taking the time to record the best performance possible, including one that is well in tune. And if the musician just can't nail the correct pitch, or the instrument has inherent pitch problems, then Auto-Tune is there for you. Of course, sometimes pitch problems remain hidden from our ears until we are in the mixing phase, when all instruments and parts that were recorded separately are now being played back together. In such situations, Auto-Tune becomes not just an important tool but a money saver, since applying pitch correction is much easier and far less expensive than bringing an artist back for another round of recording.

Which Version of Auto-Tune Do I Need?

At the time of this writing, Antares Audio Technologies offers four different flavors of Auto-Tune software and supports four different plug-in protocols for both Macintosh and Windows operating systems. Knowing which one is right for you may save you money and keep you from pulling out your hair. It is important to know that the vast majority of Auto-Tune used today is from software plug-ins that work inside of DAWs such as Avid's Pro Tools and Steinberg's Cubase. Antares also released Auto-Tune

Live in the summer of 2012, which is based heavily off of their flagship software, Auto-Tune 7. Auto-Tune Live, as its name implies, is built for live performance use and therefore has very low latency. Auto-Tune Live is covered in depth in chapter 7.

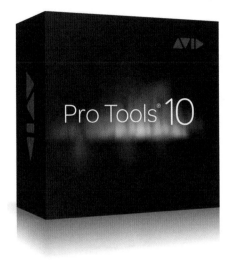

Figure 1.4

Figure 1.5

Hardware pitch correction solutions remain popular for live performance. Antares's last foray into hardware was their AVP-1, which was discontinued in 2011. That same year, Antares licensed their Auto-Tune technology to Tascam, whose TA-1VP hardware unit is an excellent and affordable solution for those wanting hardware versions of Auto-Tune. Keep in mind that all software versions of the plug-in, including Auto-Tune Live, require a computer-based DAW to be up and running during the show—a common convention to tours big and small, but one that adds complex routings to a live setup.

Figure 1.6

Auto-Tune EFX 2

Designed as a lite version of their famous software, Antares's Auto-Tune EFX 2 surfaces very few controls to the user, thereby making it very easy to use. The plug-in creates the Auto-Tune vocal effect very well, which users turn on or off via the Effect Type switch on the Auto-Tune EFX 2 interface. Auto-Tune EFX 2 is an ideal solution for music makers who only want the Auto-Tune effect or basic pitch correction in a real-time environment.

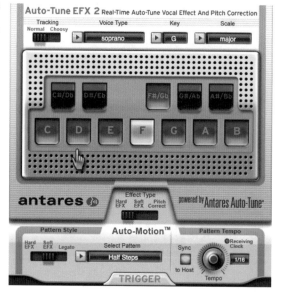

Figure 1.7

Auto-Tune EFX 2 has a new feature called Auto-Motion, which, when activated, runs the vocal through one of several melodic patterns selectable by the user. It's a bit like adding a turnaround or arpeggiation to a vocal part that did not originally have one. Auto-Motion relies on the open source MusicXML for its pattern management, and therefore requires a MusicXML editor for users wanting to create their own patterns or modify existing ones.

Auto-Tune EFX 2 is available in the native plug-in formats RTAS, AU, and VST. Typical street price is under $100.

Auto-Tune Live

Auto-Tune Live is the newest member of the Auto-Tune family. Designed for live use, Auto-Tune Live is a low-latency, Automatic-mode-only (no offline processing) solution based on the latest version of Antares's pitch correction technology. It also has deep MIDI continuous controller support. Where Auto-Tune EFX 2 offers a simple interface with few controls, Auto-Tune Live offers a comprehensive set of controls for highly professional pitch correction in a real-time environment.

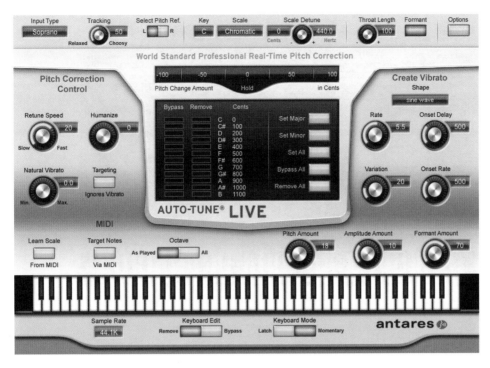

Figure 1.8

Auto-Tune Evo and Auto-Tune Version 7

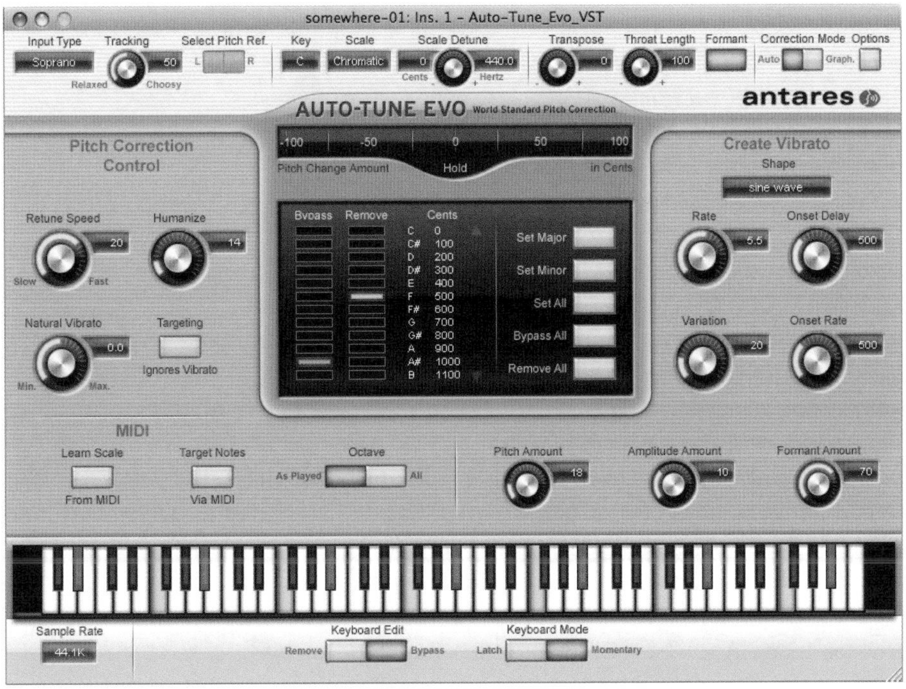

Figure 1.9

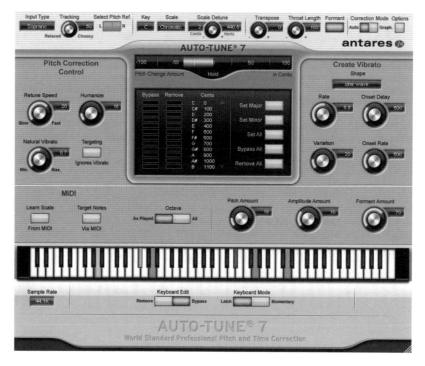

Figure 1.10

Auto-Tune Evo is the predecessor to Antares's current flagship software Auto-Tune 7. The versions are very similar but with a few key differences. First, here are features the two products share:

- Antares's Evo™ Voice Processing Technology (the latest version of the Auto-Tune algorithm).
- Automatic mode (real time) and Graphical mode (offline) support.
- Comprehensive DAW Automation Support.
- Humanization of the voice being processed.
- Vibrato control and manipulation.
- Throat modeling (preserves or augments the formant of the vocal large amounts of pitch shifting are employed).
- Real-time MIDI input in Auto mode for use in defining Target notes.
  Here are additional features only available in Auto-Tune 7:
- MIDI support in Graphical mode.
- Note-by-note throat modeling
- Time expansion and compression.

In this book, I will focus on Auto-Tune 7 because it's extremely comprehensive, powerful, and easy to use. It is also the current flagship version of the technology, and one you're likely to find in most recording studios. Mastering Auto-Tune 7 provides the skills and understanding necessary to use other Antares pitch correction products at a very high level. And since by the end of this book you will have mastered pitch correction using Auto-Tune 7, owning this flagship version is a good idea. Native versions of the software can be found for around $300 at many music stores.

Auto-Tune 7 owners can also use Auto-Tune Evo. Both versions are available in VST, AU, RTAS, and TDM formats. The TDM version does not support Auto-Tune 7's time-editing features, but the TDM version can also run as an RTAS plug-in, which does support time editing.

Chapter 2
ADDING AUTO-TUNE TO YOUR STUDIO

Adding Auto-Tune to your studio is a fairly straightforward process. The plug-in's system requirements fall well within what is recommended for today's DAWs. For Microsoft Windows systems, Windows XP is the oldest supported OS, as is Mac OS X 10.5 (Leopard) on the Apple side of things. Expect this to change in sync with new releases from Antares.

Opening Auto-Tune in your project should always be done on an audio effects insert of the track or channel that requires pitch correction. All examples, walk-throughs, and workflow discussions in this book assume that Auto-Tune has been inserted directly into the channel strip via an available channel insert.

A Bit About Bits

Auto-Tune Live is Antares's first 64-bit release, and VST and AU versions of Auto-Tune 7 are now available in 64-bit. Keep in mind that 32-bit versions usually work fine in 64-bit environments. Remember, the primary practical difference between 64-bit and 32-bit software is that 64-bit software can use more of your system's RAM. The process of installing 64-bit software versus 32-bit software is virtually identical, with a few under-the-hood differences worth noting.

Figure 2.1

Auto-Tune Installation on 32-Bit and 64-Bit Machines

On Macintosh computers, installing Auto-Tune in either 64-bit or 32-bit systems is hassle free and requires no additional steps. The software installs itself into folders based on Auto-Tune's plug-in format (AU, VST, RTAS, TDM).

Macintosh plug-in directories:

- **VST:** Macintosh HD\Library\Audio\Plug-ins\VST.
- **AU:** Macintosh HD\Library\Audio\Plugins\Components.
- **RTAS and TDM:** Macintosh HD\Library\Application Support\Digidesign\Plug-ins.

During installation on 32-bit and 64-bit Windows systems, Auto-Tune creates an Antares Audio Technologies folder plus a subfolder for the plug-in. For Auto-Tune 7, that folder is named "Auto-Tune+Time" for 32-bit installations, and "Auto-Tune 7" for 64-bit VST installations. These are considered the default locations of the plug-in, and they will not only contain the plug-in itself, but also the manual, read-me documents, and any other supporting files. In addition, the Auto-Tune installation places a copy of the plug-in in the Plug-ins folder related to the DAW and plug-in format you are using.

Whenever installing an Auto-Tune update, the installation overwrites earlier versions of the software found in the Mac and Windows default locations. If you perform a custom installation of Auto-Tune, or move the plug-in file manually through copy and paste, the Auto-Tune installer may not be able to update these files. This holds true for other plug-ins as well. Because of this, think twice before committing to a custom installation of the plug-in.

The typical default directory path to 64-bit versions of Auto-Tune 7 on a 64-bit Windows system is Program Files/Antares Audio Technologies/Auto-Tune 7 VST.

The typical default directory path to 32-bit versions of Auto-Tune 7 on a 64-bit Windows system is C:\Program Files (x86)\Antares Audio Technologies\Auto-Tune+Time VST.

The typical default directory path to 32-bit versions of Auto-Tune 7 on a 32-bit Windows system is C:\Program Files\Antares Audio Technologies\Auto-Tune+Time VST.

64-Bit Apple Logic Pro and Auto-Tune

Apple's Logic Pro, which defaults to 64-bit mode on 64-bit Macs, needs to be set to 32-bit mode in order to find and load 32-bit plug-ins. So if you plan on using 32-bit versions of Auto-Tune (or any other 32-bit plug-in) inside of 64-bit Logic Pro, you must launch Logic in 32-bit mode in order for it to scan for all 32-bit plug-ins. Once this has been done, you can switch Logic back to 64-bit mode, and Auto-Tune will remain available in Logic's list of active plug-ins. Better still, upgrade to the 64-bit AU version of Auto-Tune.

To launch Logic in 32-bit mode, you need to access Logic's Get Info window by right-clicking (or holding down the Ctrl key while left-clicking) on the Logic icon from OSX's Applications folder and selecting Get Info. Inside the Get Info window, you will find a checkbox for running the program in 32-bit mode.

Apple's Mountain Lion Gatekeeper

In summer of 2012, Apple released Mac OS X, version 10.8.x, called Mountain Lion. Mountain Lion includes Apple Gatekeeper, a new security feature that checks for an Apple-approved digital signature from apps downloaded from the Internet and not downloaded from Apple's App Store. If Gatekeeper does not find the signature, it will prevent the app's installation.

Since there is a time lag associated with adding such a feature and developers getting their digital signatures in order, there is a workaround here that, at the time of this writing, must be applied to Auto-Tune installations on Mountain Lion. Simply hold down the Control key while clicking on the Auto-Tune installer, and then click "Yes" to approve the installation, and then "Yes" to the dialog warning you that the software is from an "unknown" developer. We know the developer: it is Antares Audio Technologies, and they are working with Apple in obtaining the necessary signatures.

Mysteries of the iLok Revealed

Antares uses the iLok copy protection system to protect their software. The iLok system combines software (an online iLok.com account along with drivers and client that are installed onto your computer) and hardware (the "iLok," a USB key that stores your software licenses). The iLok's job is to protect software licenses from being exploited while allowing you, the licensee, the ability to run your software on any system you plug your iLok into. One iLok can hold 500 software licenses.

When you purchase iLok-protected software such as Auto-Tune, you must register and authorize it in order to use it. Part of the registration and authorization process includes a software license that's deposited into your online iLok account. Transfer that license from your account to your iLok USB key, and you're ready to go. The steps are simple, and as follows:

Figure 2.2

Authorizing Auto-Tune via the iLok System

1. Purchase an iLok USB key. iLoks are purchased separately and not included with Auto-Tune software. They sell for under $50 and are available at many music stores, as well as Amazon.

2. Create your iLok account. Creating your iLok account is easy. Simply plug in your iLok (ideally you should use the computer that houses your DAW), go to iLok.com, and then follow the steps offered for creating an account and installing the iLok driver and client.

   When choosing an iLok ID, select one that is memorable and not overly complicated, since it, along with your iLok password, are key to accessing your iLok account. Your iLok ID is also required when registering and authorizing Auto-Tune and any other iLok-protected software. Since the focal point of the iLok system is antipiracy, replacing a lost iLok or lost iLok account information is not trivial. You should also avoid names such as "iLok 1" or "Studio A," since they are overused and nonspecific.

3. Register your version of Auto-Tune at Antarestech.com/reg_auth/. The registration process results in a license being deposited into your iLok account. During this process, you will enter your iLok ID. It is crucial that you give the right information here, to ensure the license gets deposited properly. iLok IDs are not case sensitive.

4. Save your iLok and software registration information. As a result of the above process, you will receive e-mails from both Antares and iLok.com. You'd be smart to print these and keep them in a safe place, to serve as a backup of your iLok account information and Auto-Tune registration information. In the event that you lose an iLok or your computer dies, having this information handy will save you both time and money.

5. Install Auto-Tune with your iLok key plugged in. Before installing Auto-Tune, it's a good idea to already have your Auto-Tune license downloaded to an attached iLok, and the iLok drivers and client installed. This will simplify the iLok authorization process. If you have installed a demo version of Auto-Tune prior to setting up your iLok, any subsequent launches of the plug-in should see the license on your iLok copy, and you should be good to go. If problems occur, an Auto-Tune reinstallation is usually the easiest fix. Once installation is complete, the software should be readily available inside your DAW as long as your iLok is plugged in. Antares offers all their software available as a free download, since it cannot run beyond its demo period without a license on an attached iLok. You can find their software here: http://www.antarestech.com/download/updateform.shtml.

Figure 2.3

Auto-Tune Plug-in Formats

Auto-Tune is not a stand-alone software application. It runs as a plug-in inside DAW software such as Avid's Pro Tools or Steinberg's Cubase. Auto-Tune supports all four standard plug-in formats for pro audio software across both Mac and PC platforms.

Plug-in Format Types

- **VST:** Developed by Steinberg; VST = Virtual Studio Technology.
- **AU:** Developed by Apple and only works on Macintosh systems; AU = Audio Units.
- **RTAS:** Developed by Avid/Digidesign for Pro Tools; RTAS = Real Time AudioSuite.
- **TDM:** Also developed by Avid/Digidesign; TDM = Time Division Multiplex.

VST, AU, and RTAS are considered native formats, meaning they use the host computer's hardware for processing power. TDM is not a native format because it uses DSP hardware that is part of a Pro Tools HD TDM system. Auto-Tune in TDM format does not allow for time compression and expansion. However, the TDM version of Auto-Tune will also launch as an RTAS plug-in that does have the full suite of Auto-Tune features available.

DAW Plug-in Format Compatibility List

Here are the four primary plug-in formats and the DAWs they support. This is not a comprehensive list but instead focuses on the most popular DAW titles available.

VST

- Steinberg's Cubase, Nuendo, and Wavelab (Mac and Windows).
- Cakewalk Sonar (PC Only).
- Ableton Live (Mac and Windows; Mac version also supports AU format).
- Presonus's Studio 1 (Mac and Windows; Mac version also supports AU format).
- Adobe Audition (Mac and Windows; Mac version also supports AU).
- Sony Vegas (PC Only).

AU (Mac Only)

- Apple's Logic Pro.
- Apple's GarageBand.
- Ableton Live (VST also supported).
- Adobe Audition (VST also supported).
- MOTU's Digital Performer (RTAS also supported).
- Presonus's Studio 1.

RTAS
- Avid's Pro Tools (Mac and Windows).
- MOTU's Digital Performer (AU also supported. RTAS requires Avid's DAE software to be running).

TDM
- Avid's Pro Tools HD TDM (Mac and Windows).

Optimizing Your DAW for Auto-Tune

Auto-Tune works very well within most DAWs. There are, however, a few optimization considerations worth mentioning. Before you spend time optimizing your rig for Auto-Tune, you should have already spent time optimizing your computer for audio processing and Digital Audio Workstation use. This is especially important on PCs, which come in a myriad of different hardware configurations. It is less important for Macintosh computers, since unlike Windows systems, Apple makes both the hardware and the software for their computers. Macs are very efficient computers, and DAW optimization in OS X is really only needed if you find your projects running poorly, and even then it may be more a project size and maintenance issue as opposed to a system optimization issue.

As always, whenever making system changes to your computer—users beware! You are accessing a part of your computer where clicking on the wrong thing or incorrect adjustments could cause your computer to behave very badly (or not behave at all). When that happens, sometimes the only solution is to reinstall your operating system. Setting a restore or backup point prior to making these changes could possibly save you from reloading the OS if things go awry when accessing system settings. Now that I've suitably scared you, here are a few safe and easy optimization steps.

Safe and Easy System Optimization Steps

- Log off additional users. This takes up resources on both Mac and PC that could be better used for your project.
- Defrag your hard drive. Hard drive space is mostly a nonissue these days. Nonetheless, as you fill up your drives and create, store, and remove large amounts of data—such as audio files—your hard drive might become fragmented, causing it to perform inefficiently. Microsoft Windows includes a defrag tool available here: Start/Programs/Accessories/ System Tools. Macs are "self-optimizing," making fragmentation less of an issue. However, on drives with little free space, or drives where large amounts of data are routinely created and deleted, it's not a bad idea to invest in a third-party disc defrag tool for your Mac, since Apple does not offer one.
- Turn off the screensaver and other cute but useless programs. Having the screensaver come on during a session is awfully annoying, highly unprofessional, and a great way to cause a glitch in your audio stream. Other cute or cool-looking features, including animations, rotating desktop images, system sounds, and auto-run settings, should be shut off in order to focus resources on producing music. Think of it this way: your computer has a finite amount of resources. As the keeper of your DAW, you must decide which systems are integral to the operating system and which are little more than racing stripes—they look cool, but they don't make the thing go any faster. Always err on the side of performance.
- Turn off anything that can interrupt data streams. Printers, scanners, camera tools, auto-run settings for optical drives, and anti-virus and other security-related software are just a few of the things that can interrupt your audio work as they check to see if they are

needed or if all that data going in and out of your computer is safe. Turn these things off as much as possible. Anti-virus software can be especially problematic when running your DAW, though it is a blessing when using the Internet.

- Set your system for best performance. More assistance is offered for Windows than for Macs—and they need it. Windows 7 offers a performance troubleshooter in its control panel. Simply navigate to the control panel, type "Troubleshooter" in its search field, and follow its prompts. Focusrite and Presonus both offer excellent tips on optimizing your Windows computer for DAW use. At the time of this writing, here are the addresses where this information can be found:

  http://support.presonus.com/entries/119099-optimizing-your-computer-for-audio-windows-vista-windows-7

  http://www.focusrite.com/answerbase/en/article.php?id=1071.

Figure 2.4   Figure 2.5

Managing Multiple Instances of Auto-Tune in Large Projects

Auto-Tune 7 is not a lightweight plug-in. This is rarely a problem, except with high track-count projects employing many simultaneous instances of Auto-Tune. On native systems, there is no real workaround other than maintaining a clean system and optimizing your project as much as possible. Project optimization is often a requirement for any high track-count project, regardless of how many instances of Auto-Tune you simultaneously run.

If you run into performance issues when running multiple instances of Auto-Tune, it may be time to mix down recorded tracks into sensible groups or submixes (e.g., drums, guitars, keys). Using these submix tracks in the project while muting or disabling the individual tracks used to create them will reduce track count and free up resources for Auto-Tune while still providing a sensible level of control over the mix. Once you have Auto-Tune applied to your liking, save its settings as an Auto-Tune preset, using your DAW's plug-in preset menu appended to the top or bottom of the plug-in window, save your project, and then render/mix down the track. This is an effective way to work when you start bumping up against system resource limitations and the nasty sounds and glitches they cause. When you're ready for final mixdown, simply mute the submix tracks and revert back to the individual tracks, while keeping the successfully processed Auto-Tune tracks.

Another powerful resource-management trick is to render all virtual instrument tracks. They use a surprising amount of RAM and CPU—rendering these tracks frees up the processors to handle other tasks.

Auto-Tune in the Signal Path

All signal processors should be placed after Auto-Tune and not before it in the signal path. Reverb and other effects can interfere with Auto-Tune's ability to interpret the source audio correctly. The one exception here is compression. Placing a compressor before Auto-Tune can sometimes benefit pitch correction processing on cleanly recorded tracks. This is especially true if volume levels of the vocal part are wide ranging or inconsistent, and the vocal track does not have background noises that get noticeably boosted by the compressor. On noisy tracks, compression should be placed after any instance of Auto-Tune.

Auto-Tune and TDM

When using Auto-Tune in the Pro Tools TDM format, there is an additional tweak available to optimize resource allocation. Under the Playback Engine dialog box found in the Pro Tools Setup menu, you will find an option to select the number of voices for the session. It makes little sense to set a number much higher than what you need (keep in mind that voices include auxiliary channels and not just mixer channels). Setting Number of Voices to a value closest to your actual track count can help free DSP for TDM plug-ins. Of course, you cannot set this parameter lower than the number of tracks contained in your session.

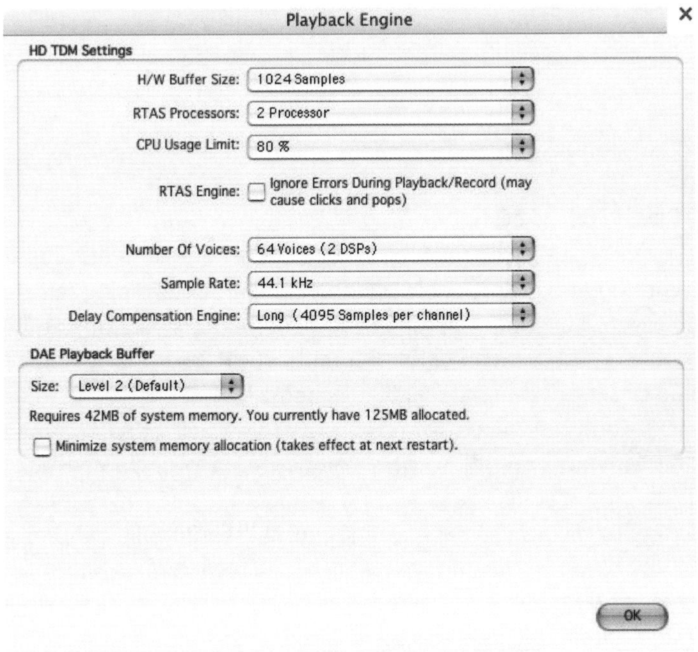

Figure 2.6

Figure 2.7

Optimizing Auto-Tune for your DAW

In most cases, Auto-Tune is ready to work upon launch. However, the plug-in offers several settings that can improve workflow while helping it conform to the limitations of your rig. Most of these settings can be found in Auto-Tune's Options dialog, accessed by clicking the Options button in the upper-right corner of the Auto-Tune window. Here's a rundown on key Options parameters, along with some tips on adjusting their values for your system.

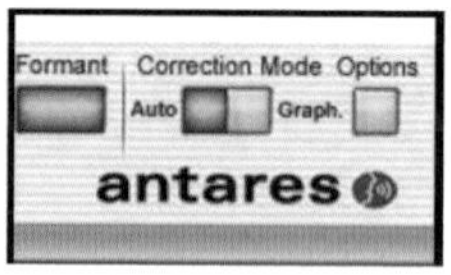

Figure 2.8

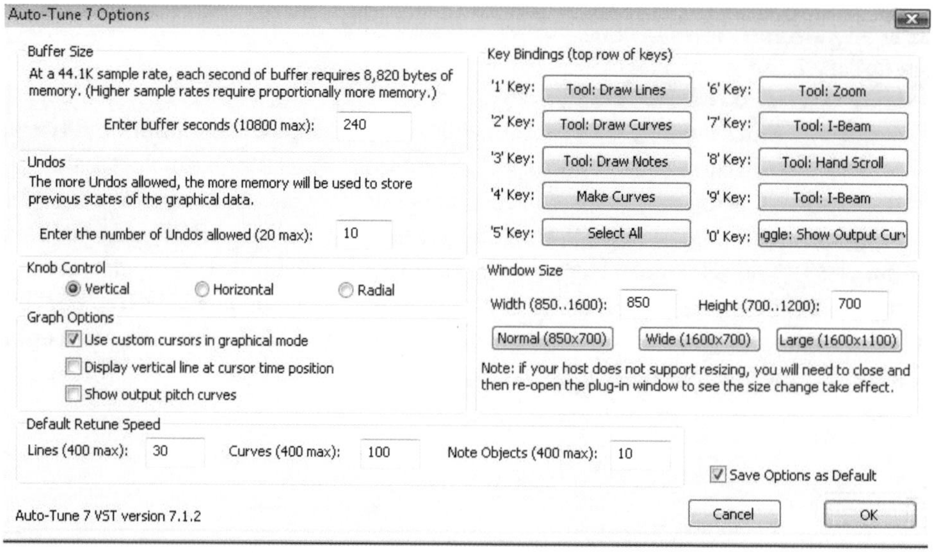

Figure 2.9

Options Dialog: Buffer Size

Auto-Tune's Graphical mode requires you play in, or "track," the audio into the plug-in prior to applying pitch correction. The Buffer Size setting in the Options dialog sets the memory buffer space (measured in seconds) permanently allocated for tracking audio. As an example, if you plan on tracking an entire 5-minute vocal part into Graphical mode, your buffer should be set to a minimum of 300 seconds.

It's best to set this important parameter to the length of your entire song, plus a few seconds to accommodate any pre-roll silences recorded into your audio tracks. Since Auto-Tune will display tracked data and its associated pitch information at the correct time relative to the project (assuming your DAW supplies valid time information to the plug-in), tracking the part you wish to pitch correct for the entire length of the song will allow you to move around the tracked audio accurately and easily. The Buffer Size's maximum setting is 14,400 seconds, or 240 minutes. The default size is 240 seconds, or 4 minutes. It needs to be set for every instance of the plug-in in your session.

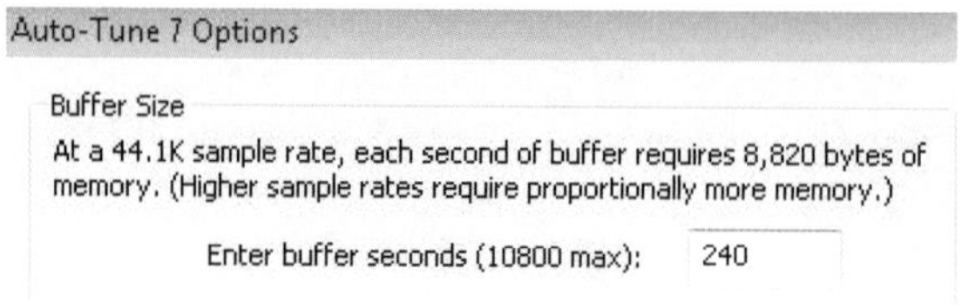

Figure 2.10

Options Dialog: Undo

Auto-Tune lets you specify the number of undo's, with a maximum of 20. This number of undo's applies independently to time expansion/compression and pitch correction and is not shared between these two processes. This function uses system memory to store the data used to perform an undo, but even at its maximum setting, this should pose no problem on today's computers. The default here is 10.

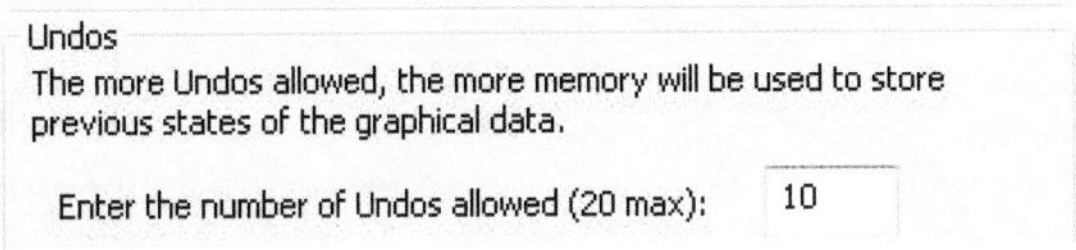

Figure 2.11

Options Dialog: Default Retune Speed

Retune Speed is the Holy Grail of parameters for getting the Auto-Tune effect. It is also a key parameter for transparent pitch correction. When you create a pitch correction object in Graphical mode, it uses the Default Retune Speed value set in the Options dialog. Each type of Correction object has its own Default Retune Speed, and setting this parameter close to the values you use the most can help improve workflow.

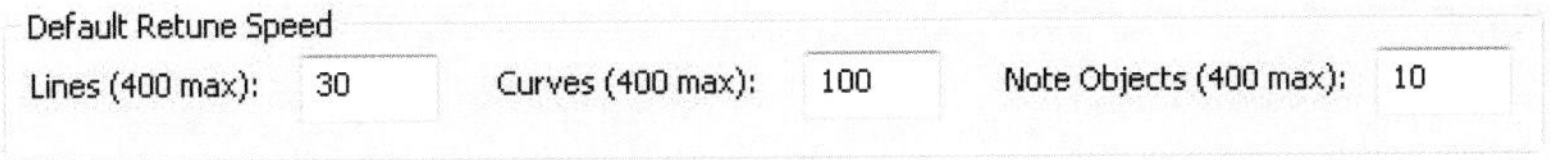

Figure 2.12

Options Dialog: Key Bindings

Professional engineers rely on shortcut keys whenever possible simply because it is an efficient way to work. Auto-Tune allows most of its tools and functions to be assigned to the 10 number keys on the QWERTY portion of your computer keyboard. With 46 different assignable tools and functions, Auto-Tune is highly customizable with regard to workflow. To assign a tool or function to a key on your keyboard, simply go to the Options dialog, locate the Key Bindings section, then click on one of the 10 button keys to assign a tool or function to that key. This, like all other settings in the Options dialog, is per instance of Auto-Tune.

Figure 2.13

Save Options as Default

At the bottom right of the Options dialog is the Save Options as Default checkbox. When checked (the default state), all future instances of Auto-Tune will open with the Options settings established in the current instance of Auto-Tune. This will come in handy once your Auto-Tune workflow takes shape.

Data File Management

Time manipulation in Auto-Tune 7 is nondestructive, and therefore, all time edits occur on copies of the original file. These copies can stack up on your hard drive. Auto-Tune 7's Graphical mode includes a Data File Management button that brings up a dialog to manage these file copies. If you perform few time edits, you will rarely need to visit this window. If you perform lots of time edits, or if hard drive space is an issue, then the Data File Management dialog can help you deal with the multiple copies

Auto-Tune has created as a result of time editing. Every instance of Auto-Tune used to perform a time edit will have its own folder for storing copies of this data.

Accessing these folders should only be done from the Data File Management dialog and not directly through your computer, since doing so can cause Auto-Tune to not find these copies when opening the session they pertain to.

In the event you need to move or archive a project that contains Auto-Tune time edits, it is important to include all associated Data File Management folders. To do this, enter a name in the File Name field found in the center of the Data File Management window, and then hit the Rename button below it. Use a sensible name that relates to the project and the instance of Auto-Tune to which it belongs, so you can easily find it and add it to the project files you are exporting.

You must save the project for any changes in the Data File Management dialog to become permanent.

If your project is finished, mixed down, and delivered, it's a good idea to delete these now useless files by clicking on the Delete button at the bottom of the Data File Management dialog (remember to save the project to save these changes).

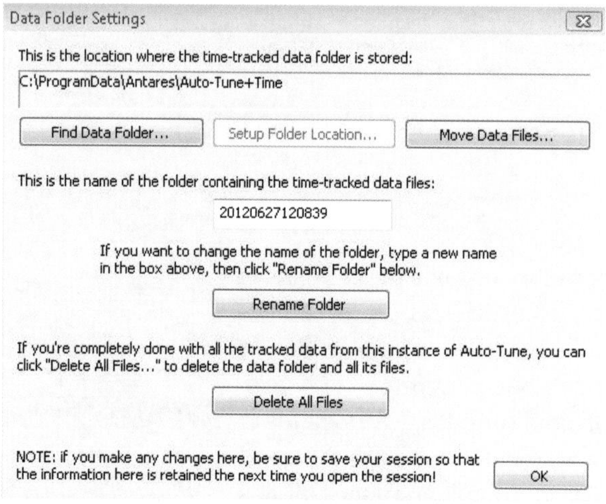

Figure 2.14

Chapter 3

THE CORRECTION MODES:
AUTOMATIC (AUTO) MODE VERSUS
GRAPHICAL (GRAPHIC) MODE

D eciding which Auto-Tune mode to work in, Automatic mode (commonly referred to as Auto mode) or Graphical mode, is the first step of the pitch correction process. Auto mode is fast and easy to use. It's an efficient way to work, especially if the source material just needs a bit of nudging to the correct pitch or if you are after the Auto-Tune vocal effect. Graphical mode, on the other hand, is highly flexible and very powerful. Both yield professional results. Auto mode allows you to apply pitch correction in a matter of seconds during playback of the mix. Graphical mode is an editing environment where you must track in the audio you are going to process.

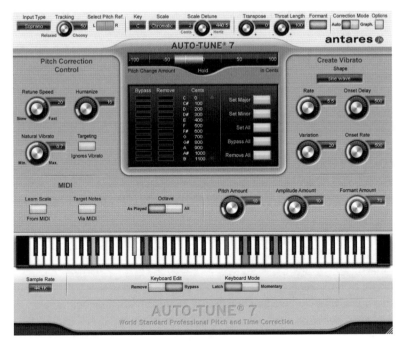

Figure 3.1

Figure 3.2

Picking the Right Correction Mode

Deciding which Auto-Tune mode is best suited for your project needs is simple. It often comes down to determining the source audio and project's pitch correction needs, the quality of the source audio recording, your preferred method of working, and the available power from your DAW.

Auto Mode Has Two Distinct Advantages over Graphical Mode

- **Fast:** Auto mode does not require tracking of audio into the plug-in prior to correction. Its processing is done online and in real time.
- **Easy:** Auto-mode pitch correction is applied globally, which simplifies workflow.

Try Auto Mode When

- The track is close to being in tune and just needs a bit of polish.
- There are no key changes in the track (this can still be handled in Auto mode via plug-in automation).
- You just want the Auto-Tune effect.
- You want real time pitch correction.
- The track is very clean and contains little or no background or incidental noises.
- You have no time for offline editing.
- You do not need surgical note-by-note manipulation of pitch, formant, or time.
- System resources are a nonissue.

Graphical Mode Has Two Distinct Advantages over Auto Mode

- **Powerful:** Surgical, note-by-note pitch processing.
- **Comprehensive:** Easy to manipulate audio data beyond preset scales and pitches.

Try Graphical Mode When

- Only certain portions of the track need pitch correction (this can also be done in Auto mode via plug-in automation).
- There are multiple key changes in the track.
- You want ultimate control over the pitch correction process.
- You need to edit melody.
- You want different types of pitch correction on a single track.
- The track is outside of traditional scales and keys offered in Auto mode.
- You need to manipulate the timing of the performance.
- Your DAW provides valid project-clock information to its plug-ins.

Trade-offs Between Auto Mode and Graphical Mode

Auto mode is an extremely fast way to work. It offers everything you need for professional pitch correction results on the fly. It also offers more control for creating vibrato. Graphical mode supports all the same correction parameters as Auto mode, but it lets you apply them on a note-by-note basis. Auto mode works on audio as it passes through the plug-in. Graphical mode only works on the portion of audio you have tracked and applied pitch correction objects to. Principle pitch parameters such as Tracking, Key, and Scale are shared between these two modes. It's how these and other parameters are applied that define the key differences between these two modes. Graphical mode is certainly the deep end of the pool, and those new to the technology will have an easier time of it starting with Auto mode.

Auto Mode and Real Time Pitch Correction

Even though Auto-Tune 7's Auto mode is designed for real-time usage, the plug-in is not specifically designed for "live" use. If you must use Auto-Tune software live and your vocalist insists on monitoring or recording his or her performance with Auto-Tune in the signal path (this is not recommended), and you as the engineer or producer have accepted the trade-offs of this workflow methodology, then consider using the new Auto-Tune Live, or Auto-Tune EFX 2. Hardware versions of the technology such as TASCAM's TA-1VP are also viable solutions for live use.

Lowering audio buffer sizes (which in turn lowers latency) can greatly improve real-time tracking and monitoring with Auto-Tune software; doing so increases the resource requirements for your DAW. If your computer cannot handle the additional strain caused by this, audio dropouts and glitches can result. See the section "Managing Multiple Instances of Auto-Tune in Large Projects" in chapter 2 to learn how to get around this problem.

Figure 3.3

Auto Mode and Graphical Mode Working Together

Starting in Auto mode is a great way to learn Auto-Tune and make progress quickly. As you gain more experience with the software, transitioning to Graphical mode will happen naturally. Auto-Tune helps facilitate this transition by letting you import your Auto mode settings into Graphical mode. This is not only a great way to manage the Auto-Tune learning curve, it is also a great way to work. As you dial in pitch correction using Auto mode, you may begin to hear places in the audio track where a more detailed use of pitch correction is needed, or where a section of the vocal sounds better unprocessed, or where the part needs pitch correction outside the scale or key set in Auto mode. Whatever the reason, the more you work in Auto mode, the better you will be able to discern when your audio can use a bit of surgical pitch correction courtesy of Graphical mode. In chapter 6, you'll learn how easy it is to use Auto mode and Graphical mode together, which is a great way to get your feet wet in the deep end of the Auto-Tune pool.

Chapter 4

MASTERING PITCH CORRECTION IN AUTOMATIC MODE

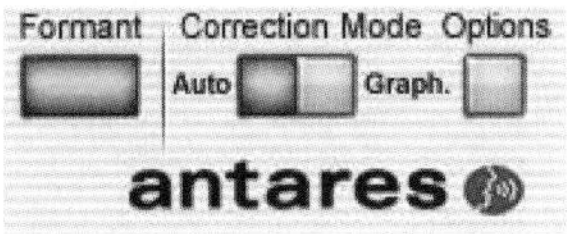

A uto-Tune's two different correction modes, Automatic mode and Graphical mode, are selected by clicking on their respective buttons in the top right of the Auto-Tune display.

Auto mode in Auto-Tune works much like any other real-time plug-in. Source audio comes into the plug-in, Auto-Tune monitors it in real time in order to detect its various pitches, and pitch correction is then applied based on the parameters you've set. The resulting output is either an in-tune version of the source audio, or an effected version of the source audio (the Auto-Tune effect). This happens very fast so as not to interfere with the timing of your mix. If you're using Auto-Tune Live, it is fast enough for real-time "live" use.

Figure 4.1

A Tour of Auto Mode's Controls

Let's walk through the Auto mode parameters, focusing on the ones that get used the most. Parameters and features given their own chapters, such as vibrato and MIDI, will be identified, but not in detail for obvious reasons (i.e., see their respective chapters!)

Input Type

Setting the Input Type focuses Auto-Tune's audio source monitoring to specific frequencies or pitches. For example, if you set Input Type to Bass Instrument, then the plug-in knows to look for low-end frequencies (as low as 25 Hertz, which is much lower than a human can sing). If you set it to Soprano, it knows to ignore low frequencies and focus instead on higher pitches found in the human voice. Along with Tracking knob adjustments (described below), setting the correct Input Type also helps Auto-Tune ignore incidental noises, such as the higher pitch sound of a plectrum on a bass guitar string or a foot stomp accidentally picked up by a vocalist's microphone. For vocal parts with a wide pitch range, Alto/Tenor Voice is usually ideal.

Figure 4.2

Input Types:
- Soprano Voice
- Alto/Tenor Voice
- Low Male Voice
- Instrument
- Bass Instrument

Tracking

The Tracking parameter controls how selective Auto-Tune will be in detecting pitches in the source audio that can then be corrected. This is an important parameter, since pitch detection must occur before pitch correction can take place. The Tracking knob adjusts how much variance there can be in the waveform before two cycles are considered identical, which is the criteria Auto-

Figure 4.3

Tune uses to identify pitch. The default is 50, which is halfway between its maximum settings for Relaxed and Choosy. Auto-Tune's pitch detection technology has improved so much over the years that adjusting this parameter should be a rare event.

On tracks with lots of background noises (such as live recordings), and tracks where the vocalist's breath or physical movements have been prominently picked up by the microphone, use your DAW's editing tools to remove as many of these noises from the track as possible before applying Auto-Tune. Running the track through Auto mode first with Input Type, Tracking, and Scale and Key set correctly can help you find areas where noises in the track can impede the pitch correction process. Noisy audio tracks are also excellent candidates for Auto-Tune's Graphical mode.

Tracking Parameters range from 100 (maximum Relaxed) to 1(maximum Choosy). It's worth restating that while this is an important parameter, it's often best to leave it at its default setting of 50 and then reach for it if pitch detection becomes problematic, which can manifest as pops and clicks during playback in Auto mode (too Relaxed), or notes not receiving pitch correction (too Choosy).

Key and Scale

Setting the correct key is, pardon the pun, key to effective pitch correction results in Auto mode. Same goes for setting the correct scale. When you click the Key and Scale parameters in Auto-Tune, menus will appear, allowing you to select the best key and scale for your project. Notes from this selection will be shown in the Edit Scale display (described below).

Auto-Tune offers 29 different scales, including chromatic, which includes all notes regardless of selected key. If your source material is only sharp or flat by a few cents (or less than half a semitone), then setting the scale to Chromatic can yield good results, as this will correct all pitches to the closest semitone. You can alter any scale simply by clicking a note's Bypass or Remove button in the Edit Scale display, as described below.

Figure 4.4

Target Notes

Selecting a key and scale sets the notes Auto-Tune will pitch correct to in Auto mode. These are called Target notes, and they will appear in the Edit Scale display where, as you will soon see, they can be manipulated.

Scale Detune

All scales and keys in Auto mode assume the reference pitch of A = 440 Hertz. This means all keys are based on A above middle C being tuned to 440 Hertz, or 440 cycles per second, the standard reference pitch for most Western music. However, music is often recorded at reference pitches above and below A = 440 Hertz. If the music accompanying the tracks you wish to pitch correct does not conform to the A = 440 Hertz reference pitch, use the Scale Detune knob to adjust Auto-Tune's scales and keys to the reference pitch of your music. The range of this parameter is plus or minus 100 cents (one semitone).

Figure 4.5

Using Scale Detune to Determine Your Song's Reference Pitch

If you don't know the song's reference pitch, but you know it's not A = 440, here's how Auto-Tune can help. Simply set Auto-Tune's scale to Chromatic, then find a constant monophonic tone in the project suitable for use as a reference frequency (bass or keyboard notes work well here, vocals do not—it does not need to be a very long section). Set your DAW to loop that section, and then run it through Auto-Tune using Auto mode. Adjust the Scale Detune parameter until the Pitch Change Amount Meter stays at or close to 0. This sets Scale Detune to match the reference frequency of your song.

Transpose

Where Scale Detune changes the reference pitch of the scales and keys in Auto-Tune, Transpose changes the pitch, by semitones, of the source audio itself. For many Transpose adjustments, you should use the Formant button to preserve the transposed audio's formants.

Figure 4.6

Formant

The formants of the human voice are what give it its distinct resonance and character. In short, formants are, in part, what makes Rod Stewart sound like Rod Stewart and Aretha Franklin sound like the Queen of Soul. Use the Formant button in Auto-Tune to keep large changes in pitch (usually a full step or greater) sounding natural. Without this parameter, large changes in pitch (either from the correction process or from using the Transpose feature) can sound unrealistic, as if chipmunks or giants are singing your song.

Throat Length

The physical shape of a singer's throat has a lot to do with his or her vocal characteristics. Auto-Tune's Throat Length control lets you modify the characteristics of a vocal performance based on throat length. It can make a female vocal part sound male, and vice versa. It can also be used for special effects. Moving the Throat Length knob to the right increases throat length, and moving it to the left decreases it. Small changes with this parameter are best, in order to preserve a realistic sound. The best way to understand this knob is to tweak while playing audio through Auto mode. To engage Throat Length, you must first click on the Formant button. In Graphical mode, Throat Length can be applied on a note-by-note basis.

Pitch Change Amount Indicator

This meter shows how much pitch correction is being applied. It is a good way to validate that you are using the best key and scale possible for the track using Auto-Tune. It also shows you how out of tune the source audio is. If you see this meter really pumping,

Figure 4.7

than most likely the part is wildly out of tune, your pitch correction needs are drastic, or Auto mode's pitch correction parameters are not set optimally (as in, you are not correcting to the best scale and key for the song). Later in this chapter, you will learn how to use Auto mode to determine the ideal Key and Scale settings for your project. Using Auto mode to determine the best Scale Detune settings was already covered in the preceding paragraphs.

Edit Scale Display

This window shows you the Target notes in your selected key and scale, and gives you control over them. Each Target note shown in this window can be bypassed or removed from the scale by clicking its respective Bypass or Remove button. For any non-diatonic scale, Set Major and Set Minor buttons will also appear in the Edit Scale display. Here's a list of the controls found here.

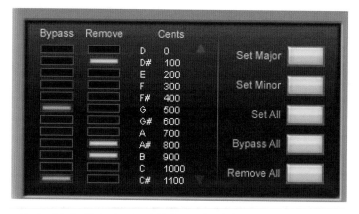

Figure 4.8

- **Bypass:** Any source material close to a Target note set to bypass will be output at its original pitch and not processed by Auto-Tune.
- **Remove:** Removed notes are removed from the current scale, forcing Auto-Tune to use the next closest note in that scale to correct to. For example, if you remove F# from an E minor scale, then any notes close to F# will be corrected to G if sharper than F#, or E if flatter than F#.

- **Bypass All:** Clicking this bypasses all Target notes in the currently selected scale, which you can then select on a note-by-note basis by clicking on an individual note's Bypass button.
- **Remove All:** Clicking this removes all Target notes in the currently selected scale, which you can then select on a per-note basis by clicking on an individual note's Remove button.
- **Set Major:** Clicking Set Major will remove all notes of the currently selected key and scale that are not part of a major scale.
- **Set Minor:** Clicking Set Minor will remove all notes of the currently selected key and scale that are not part of a minor scale.
- **Set All:** Click Set All to reset Bypass and Remove filters.

All adjustments in the Edit Scale display affect all octaves. To focus scale edits to a specific octave, use the Virtual Keyboard at the bottom of the Auto-Tune Auto mode window.

Virtual Keyboard, Keyboard Edit, and Keyboard Mode

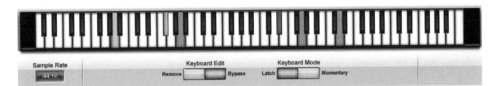

Figure 4.9

At the bottom of the Auto mode window is an 88-key Virtual Keyboard, available as both a reference tool and an editing tool. When audio is running through Auto-Tune's Auto mode, keys on this keyboard will turn blue to show you the detected incoming pitches—a great reference for helping you find the key and scale of your music if you do not know it. In addition, you can click on keys on this keyboard in order to bypass or remove notes in the selected scale. This is similar to Bypass and Remove in the Edit Scale display with one important distinction. When using the Edit Scale display, Bypass and Remove settings affect all octaves. Bypass a G, and G notes in all octaves are bypassed. The Virtual Keyboard, on the other hand, bypasses or removes only the specific notes you have clicked on. Click the G♯ below middle C on Auto mode's Virtual Keyboard, and only that instance of G♯ is affected. Whether selected notes are removed or bypassed here depends on the Keyboard Edit setting located below the Virtual Keyboard. This is where you select either Remove or Bypass for Virtual Keyboard editing. Similar to the Edit Scale display, scales established using the Virtual Keyboard can include both removed and bypassed notes. Just select one or the other using the Keyboard Edit selector. The Virtual Keyboard is only available for editing when a scale containing 12 notes has been selected. Therefore, if you wish to edit a major or minor scale using the Virtual Keyboard, select Chromatic from the Scale menu, then use Set Major or Set Minor from the Edit Scale display.

Latch Mode and Momentary Mode

The Virtual Keyboard has two editing modes, Latch mode and Momentary mode. Select one or the other under the Keyboard mode section just below the Virtual Keyboard itself. The default mode is Latch mode, which employs the typical behavior of a mouse button press (single-clicking any key on the Virtual Keyboard selects or deselects that key). Momentary mode selects any key you've clicked on only for as long as you hold the mouse button down, making it suitable for "riding" notes while audio is running through Auto-Tune's Auto mode.

Lastly, the Virtual Keyboard uses color coding to show you the state of any key. Virtual Keyboard color codes:

- **Blue:** Detected pitches of the source audio.
- **Gray:** Notes removed from the scale.
- **Brown:** Notes bypassed from the scale.

The Pitch Correction Control Section

Figure 4.10

You've set your key and your scale, edited them as necessary, and hit Play on the transport of your DAW. You are already pitch correcting, good for you. Now let's make it better. Pitch correction as a tool and as an effect is primarily determined by adjustments in the Pitch Correction Control section.

A Tour of the Pitch Control Section Parameters

Here is a tour of the Pitch Control section parameters:

- **Retune Speed:** This parameter is arguably the single-most important control in Auto-Tune. Setting it correctly provides both transparent pitch correction and the Auto-Tune vocal effect. Retune Speed values are in milliseconds from 0 to 400. Turn the Retune Speed knob clockwise to lower its value (increase its speed), and turn it counterclockwise to increase its value (decrease its speed). While this parameter is of supreme importance for all forms of pitch correction, it remains a simple one to use and master. Retune Speed is in many ways the man behind the curtain in Auto-Tune's Oz.
- **Humanize:** Transparent pitch correction would not exist in Auto mode if it were not for Auto-Tune's powerful Humanize parameter. In the next section, you will learn how both Retune Speed and Humanize work together. Humanize values range from 0 (off), to 100.
- **Natural Vibrato:** The Natural Vibrato knob works on vibrato present in the performance you're applying pitch correction to. Its goal is to decrease or increase the width of that vibrato (width = the distance between the low and high pitches in the vibrato). Its default state is 0 (off). This parameter is independent of Auto-Tune's pitch correction parameters.

- **Targeting Ignores Vibrato:** Auto-Tune can sometimes attempt to pitch correct wide vibrato performances to two different notes (the low and high notes of the vibrato). This can cause an unnatural warbling sound. If turning on this button helps, then great! If not, then adjusting Natural Vibrato or using Graphical mode are viable alternatives. This parameter acts independently of pitch correction parameters.

Using Auto Mode for Transparent, Professional Pitch Correction

As you've learned, Graphical mode is where Auto-Tune flexes its muscles. But Auto mode is there for a reason, and sometimes that reason is speed. Here's how Auto mode can quickly provide professional, transparent pitch correction.

It's All About Retune Speed

For natural pitch correction, Retune Speed settings between 20 (the default setting) and 50 are usually ideal. Retune Speed requires a bit of tweaking in order to find the ideal setting for transparent pitch correction. The vocal style and technique found in the source audio has as much to do with how Retune Speed should be set as does the duration of notes. For highly stylized vocals and parts featuring a high number of elongated notes, increasing Retune Speed is often called for. Especially in rock and blues performances where singers tend to reach for or bend to the right note instead of hitting it dead on. However, you may find that as you increase the Retune Speed amount, short notes may not get properly corrected. Conversely you may find that shorter Retune Speed amounts can result in long notes sounding unnaturally static as Auto-Tune locks them down to the correct pitch. Reconciling these different correction requirements is where the Humanize parameter comes into play.

Humanizing Pitch Correction

Properly setting the Humanize control, just like properly setting Retune Speed, is critical to achieving natural-sounding pitch correction results in Auto mode. Humanize allows you to set relatively short Retune Speed values while preventing Auto-Tune from overprocessing long notes that, by their nature, contain slight variances in pitch that are an endemic part of singing. Here's how to use Retune Speed and Humanize together for transparent pitch correction.

First dial in Retune Speed for the shorter notes in your source audio. (Humanize should be set to 0 while dialing in Retune Speed.) Setting Retune Speed in this way will probably result in the longer notes of the source audio not sounding realistic. Now, start bringing up the Humanize knob until these longer notes regain their natural characteristics while still being properly pitch corrected. What Humanize is doing here is slowing the Retune Speed for these longer notes.

If some of your longer notes are not getting pitch corrected properly, you've probably set Humanize too high. In this case, scale back Humanize while adjusting (usually increasing by small amounts) Retune Speed until you find the right balance between the two parameters. By following the above workflow, you should end up with short notes that get pitch corrected properly, and long notes that preserve their character and yet still receive subtle but appropriate amounts of pitch correction. In other words, dialing in Retune Speed in tandem with Humanize is the key to natural-sounding, transparent pitch correction in Auto mode. As with many of Auto mode's parameters, let your ears, not your eyes, be your guide.

Keeping Natural Vibrato Natural

Preserving a singer's vibrato is not only an important aspect of natural-sounding pitch correction, it is a prerequisite if you ever want to work with the same singer more than once. The challenge with vibrato present in a performance is that if it contains wide variances in pitch, or if it is not well honed, Auto-Tune can interpret it as an out-of-tune part and try to pitch correct it. This results in either a flattening of the vibrato or an unmusical warble. Setting Natural Vibrato correctly addresses these issues.

For vocal parts where the vibrato is so wide that Auto-Tune tries to pitch correct it to two different notes, or it simply no longer sits well in the track in relation to the pitch correction processing surrounding it, try decreasing the Natural Vibrato parameter. Doing so decreases the width of the vibrato. If Auto-Tune is flattening the vibrato to a single note, increase the Natural Vibrato knob. In both instances, a little goes a long way.

Also, using the Edit Scale display to remove or bypass notes that are present in the vibrato can help tame a wide vibrato performance. The trade-off here is that any bypassed or removed notes will also have an impact on pitch correcting the rest of the track. While plug-in automation can help here, if this method saves the vibrato but hurts the rest of the track, then the track is probably best suited for Graphical mode pitch correction.

The Create Vibrato Section

Figure 4.11

This section of Auto-mode is designed to emulate vibrato when it has been either removed from the source audio via the pitch correction process (though really, this should rarely ever happen if you have done your work dialing in transparent pitch correction), or it was not there to begin with but you wish it were. Look to chapter 8 for more about the controls found in this section.

A Tour of the Create Vibrato Section Controls

- **Shape:** This drop-down menu offers standard wave shapes of sine, square, and sawtooth for creating a vibrato effect. Sine most closely resembles a naturally sung vibrato. Square offers a very pronounced effect. Setting this parameter also turns on the Create Vibrato section.
- **Rate:** Rate sets the vibrato's speed. Its default is 5.5 Hertz with a range from 0.1 Hertz to 10 Hertz.

- **Variation:** This parameter attempts to humanize Auto-Tune's Create Vibrato feature by adding small inconsistencies to the created vibrato's pitch, amplitude, and rate. The default is 20, which works fine in most cases. The range is from 0 (no variation) to 100.
- **Onset Delay:** Singers often use vibrato at the tail of long notes. Onset Delay allows you to set a delay time before the vibrato effect is applied, in order to emulate how singers commonly use vibrato. Onset Delay's values are in milliseconds, with a range from 0 (no onset delay) to 1500 (1.5 seconds).
- **Onset Rate:** Vibrato often starts subtly and then increases for dramatic effect. Onset Rate helps simulate this technique. Onset Rate is the amount of time between the end of the Onset Delay and the full effect of vibrato as defined by the Pitch, Amplitude and Formant parameters in the Create Vibrato section.
- **Pitch Amount:** Pitch Amount sets the width of the pitch changes in the vibratos you create in Auto-Tune. The range is from 0 (no change) to 100. Less is more here when creating natural-sounding vibrato.
- **Amplitude Amount:** Amplitude amount adjusts the amount of volume change in the vibrato effect. The default setting is 10 and works fine in most instances. The range is 0 (no change in amplitude) to 30 (maximum change in amplitude). At high values, this can introduce a tremolo effect, which can be quite interesting on instrument tracks.
- **Formant Amount:** As you will see when experimenting with this control, subtle formant changes are key to a natural-sounding vibrato. The range of this knob is from 0 (no formant changes) to 100 (maximum formant change). It works on the resonant timbre detected in the source audio. The default is 70, which is an ideal amount in most applications.

MIDI and Auto Mode

Auto mode is a great mode for working in MIDI, as you will see in chapter 9, which is dedicated entirely to using MIDI and Auto-Tune together. For the Auto-Tune effect, incoming MIDI data can also be used to help edit melody or create a new melody from the audio being processed by Auto-Tune.

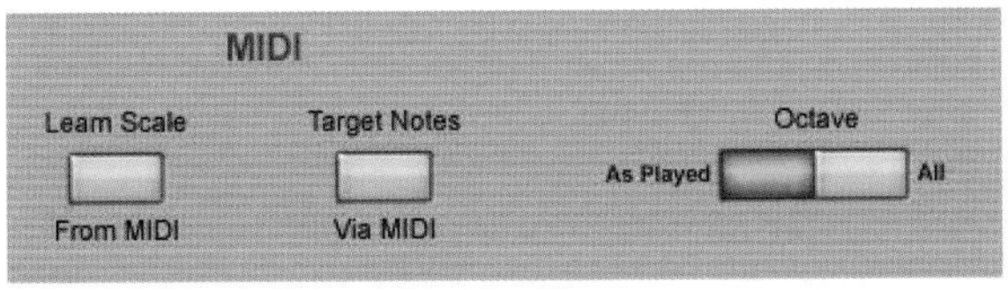

Figure 4.12

A Tour of the Auto-Mode MIDI Controls
- **Learn Scale From MIDI:** This feature allows you to create a custom scale or series of Target notes in Auto-Tune by playing MIDI data into the plug-in.
- **Target Notes Via MIDI:** This setting is quite similar to Learn Scale From MIDI, with one key difference. Target Notes Via MIDI does not establish a scale. It is designed for real-time input into Auto-Tune. And once the MIDI notes stop playing, Auto-Tune no longer makes them available as pitch correction Target notes.
- **Octave as Played/All Octaves:** Choosing All Octaves means the notes played in via MIDI will be set for all octaves, not just the ones that contained them.

Chapter 5

THE POWER OF GRAPHICAL MODE

A s you will soon see, Graphical mode is really where the power of pitch correction comes to life. And while the Graphical mode interface may look daunting at first, it's actually highly intuitive.

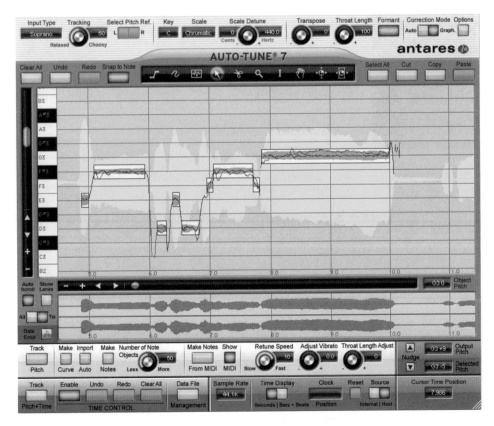

Figure 5.1

This chapter assumes you have already grasped the concepts expressed in the previous chapter, "Mastering Pitch Correction in Auto Mode," and you already have a solid understanding of the Auto mode parameters as explained in that chapter.

Graphical Mode Housekeeping

New instances of Auto-Tune always open in Auto mode. If you are not already in Graphical mode, click on the Graphical mode button on the upper right of the Auto mode display to enter Graphical mode.

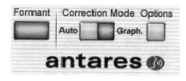

Figure 5.2

It should also be obvious by now that Auto-Tune should always be opened as an audio insert on the track requiring pitch correction.

Figure 5.3

Before tracking audio into Graphical mode, there are a few housekeeping items to be aware of that, when taken care of up front, can optimize the workflow and precision Graphical mode accommodates.

Clock Source and Clock Display

In most cases, your DAW will send project clock information to Auto-Tune. Most major DAWs, including Pro Tools, Cubase, Nuendo, and Logic, do this automatically. This makes navigating around Graphical mode's Pitch Graph display a breeze, since tracked audio displayed in Graphical mode will remain in sync with your project. In these cases, you want to make sure the clock Source located in the Clock section beneath the Pitch Graph display is set to Host.

Figure 5.4

If your DAW does not send valid time information to its plug-ins, then Source should be set to Internal. This setting forces Auto-Tune to use its own internal clock for playback of audio tracked into Graphical mode. It also forces you, the Auto-Tune user, to start playback at the exact same place you started tracking audio into Graphical mode. And to stop playback (and to stop tracking audio), you will need to hit the Reset button, also located in Graphical mode's Clock section.

The Clock display (to the left of the Source buttons) shows the current time value of tracked audio during playback. If, during playback, this data is not being updated correctly when compared to your DAW's own project clock display, then your DAW is not sending valid (or any) time data to the plug-in. In such cases you must set Source to Internal and start and stop playback per the above paragraph. You may want to contact your DAW's technical support department or search their support documentation to make sure this is not due to a setting inside the DAW itself. Not being able to use the Host clock setting in Auto-Tune can impede workflow. Another downside to having to use Auto-Tune's internal clock instead of your DAW's is that you cannot use multiple instances of Auto-Tune in Graphical mode without the plug-in being displayed.

Keep in mind that even when valid clock information is being sent to the plug-in, your DAW's project clock and Auto-Tune's Graphical mode Clock Position may not always match 100 percent during playback or tracking. Any differences here should be quite small (usually less than 1 millisecond) and no cause for alarm. If Auto-Tune keeps tracking or playing when DAW playback has been stopped, it is safe to assume no valid clock information is being sent to the plug-in, and the Internal clock setting must be used.

As we learn about Graphical mode, this chapter assumes you are able to use the Host clock setting in Auto-Tune, and if you can't, you now know how to adapt to the constraints of the Internal clock setting.

Buffer Size

This is not located in the Graphical mode window but rather in the Options dialog. As covered in chapter 2, make sure you have set the Buffer Size to accommodate the length of the audio you will be tracking into Graphical mode, plus a few seconds.

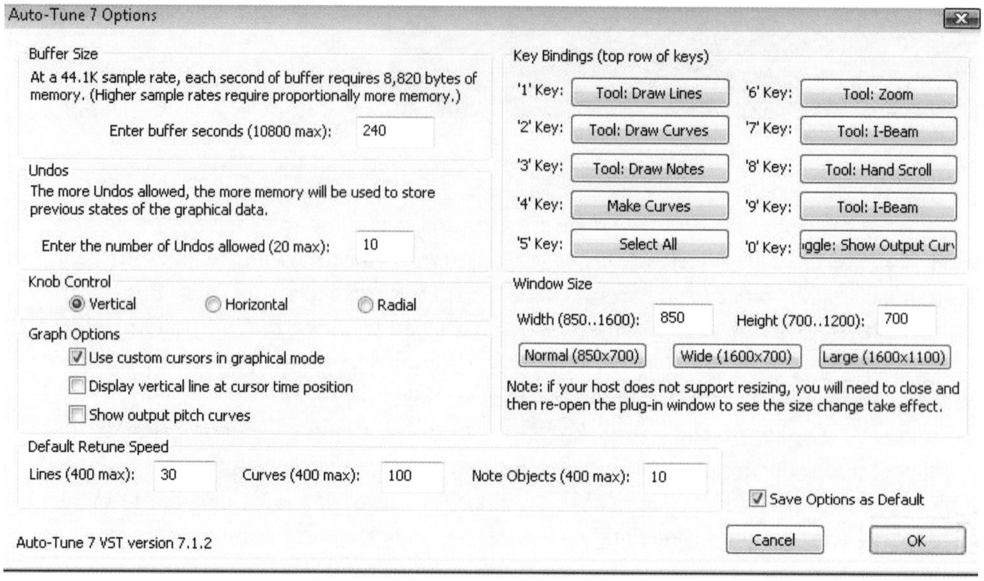

Figure 5.5

Default Retune Speed

The power of Graphical mode lies in its ability to set pitch correction parameters on a per-object basis. This includes allowing a different Retune Speed for every note or section you plan on pitch correcting.

To maximize workflow, Auto-Tune offers in its Options dialog a Default Retune Speed amount for each of the three types of Correction objects available in Graphical mode: curves, lines, and notes. The defaults are set differently based on certain workflow assumptions. It assumes that when working with Note objects, your goal is the Auto-Tune/Cher/T-Pain effect (Note objects are an excellent choice here); when working with Line objects, your goal is typical pitch correction, similar to the defaults found in Auto mode; and for Curve objects, your goal is subtle and highly transparent pitch correction and surgically precise pitch editing. This may or may not fit with how you use Graphical mode. Since Retune Speed can be changed on a per-Correction-object basis for now, let's keep to the defaults established in the Options dialog. The more you use Auto-Tune, the better grasp you will have on what Retune Speed defaults work best for you.

Life Inside the Pitch Graph Display

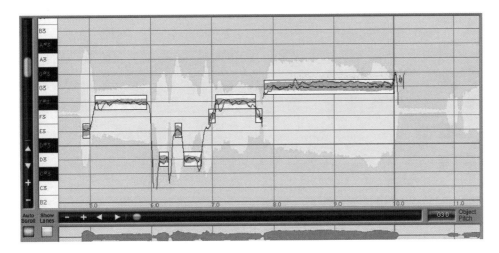

Figure 5.6

This window is at the heart of what Graphical mode is all about. Here you will select portions of tracked audio for pitch correction, analyze pitches for correction requirements, and apply pitch correction by creating and manipulating Correction objects. Audio tracked into Graphical mode is shown as an amplitude waveform in this display and in the Envelope Graph display described below.

The Time and Pitch Axes

The horizontal axis of the Pitch Graph display shows time—where you are in your tracked audio, and where you are in relationship to your project's time (assuming your DAW supports that, as discussed previously). The vertical axis shows pitch. An apt comparison of this axis would be to that of a piano keyboard. Look closely at this vertical bar, and you will see traditional note names along with their octave numbers (G#3, B-1, etc.). Note and octave text may not be shown when zoomed out, so zoom in (described below) if they are not visible.

Both axes have plus or minus zoom buttons. For the horizontal axis, these buttons zoom the tracked audio's waveform in or out based on time, much like the horizontal zoom buttons of your DAW's project or track window. If not already present, a slider will appear when zooming in, so you can adjust what portion of the waveform is present in the Pitch Graph display (again, this is similar to a horizontal slider in your DAW's track or project window). This does not move the actual audio you have tracked. It only moves what is visible in the Pitch Graph display.

The vertical axis zoom buttons zoom the pitch graph reference lanes or lines (commonly referenced in this book as note lanes or note lines) in or out. The notes found in the vertical axis are independent of the waveform, and are merely a reference for analyzing the original pitch of the tracked audio and manipulating and placing pitch correction objects. When you zoom in or out on the pitch axis, you are adjusting how many note lines are visible in the Pitch Graph display at any one time. Moving the vertical scroll bar moves these pitches up and down over the tracked audio. This pitch reference mechanism will become more apparent as you begin applying pitch correction in Graphical mode.

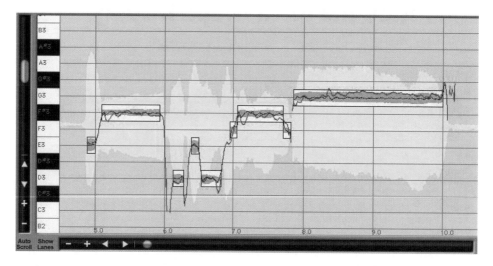

Figure 5.7

Time Display

Vertical lines in the Pitch Graph display mark time in bars and beats or in seconds. You can toggle between these two settings using the Time display buttons located to the left of the Clock Position window in Graphical mode. These time markers are a lot more useful if your DAW sends valid clock data to Auto-Tune. Setting this to match the clock mode in your DAW is usually a good idea.

Pitch Reference Lines and Lanes

The default Pitch Graph display uses lines as a reference for note values (technically called Pitch Reference Lines). Stemming from the vertical pitch axis, they create a pitch graph overlay for the tracked audio's waveform. When using major or minor scales (the two most common scales in popular Western music), pitch graph lines will be blue if they are not part of the selected scale, and dark gray if they are.

If you are working with Note objects instead of curves, you may find it easier to have Auto-Tune show lanes instead of lines for this pitch graph overlay. Click Show Lanes, located to the left of the Envelope Graph display, to engage this feature. Show Lanes is only available for major, minor, and chromatic scales. Note lanes are not color coded based on the current scale. Instead they will be gray for sharps or flats, similar to the black keys on a piano, and white for natural notes, similar to the white keys on a piano.

Auto Scroll

This is turned on by default, causing Auto-Tune to scroll the tracked audio during playback and tracking. Auto Scroll makes it easy to keep track of where you are in the project during playback. If Auto Scroll is selected when you track audio (the default state), Auto-Tune will show the entire tracked waveform in the Pitch Graph display upon the completion of tracking. It's best to leave Auto Scroll on as we walk through tracking audio and correcting pitch in Graphical mode.

Figure 5.8

Envelope Graph Display

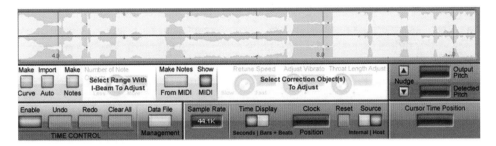

Figure 5.9

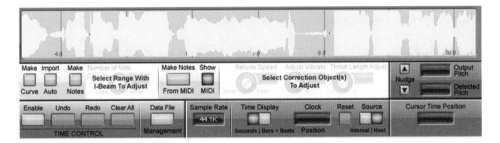

Figure 5.10

Below the Pitch Graph display is the Envelope Graph display, which shows the entire amplitude waveform of the audio tracked in Graphical mode. The default state for Graphical mode in Auto-Tune 7 has Track Pitch + Time enabled, which causes two identical instances of the amplitude waveform to be displayed in the Envelope Graph display. (The reason for this is covered in chapter 12.) Turning Enable off resets the Envelope Graph display to a single track view.

All/Tie

The All and Tie buttons toggle between two available display states for the Envelope Graph display. When All is selected, the amplitude waveform in the Envelope Graph display is shown for the entire tracked audio. This is preferred in most cases, and it's best to start with it set this way. When Tie is selected, the Envelope Graph display is "tied" to the Pitch Graph display, and therefore shows only the portion of the waveform displayed in the Pitch Graph display.

Parameters Shared Between Auto Mode and Graphical Mode

Figure 5.11

The parameters across the very top of the Graphical mode window should look very familiar, since they are also at the top of the Auto mode window. These parameters are shared between Auto mode and Graphical mode, though their behavior within these modes can be different. Input Type, Tracking, Transpose, Throat Length, and Formant work the same in both modes, in that they globally affect the audio being processed, as described in chapter 4. With two exceptions, Scale and Key only affect the display of Pitch Reference Lines or lanes on the Pitch Graph display's vertical axis. The exceptions here are that Scale and Key also play a role when creating Note objects automatically, using the Make Notes button or the Number of Note Objects knob, and when creating Curve objects using Graphical mode's Import Auto feature. In these instances, Note or Curve Correction objects are created in the Pitch Graph display based on these global Key and Scale parameters. Lastly, Scale Detune—which, as discussed in chapter 4, adjusts Auto-Tune's reference pitch from the standard A = 440 Hertz—only affects the position of Pitch Reference Lines or lanes relative to its setting.

You should already have a thorough understanding of these shared parameters, since they were covered in depth in the previous chapter.

Tracking Audio for Pitch Correction

Understanding the power of Graphical mode is best served if you have tracked audio into Graphical mode's Pitch Graph display. To accommodate this, open Auto-Tune in your DAW as an audio insert on the track you wish to pitch correct. Enter Graphical mode by clicking the Graph button in the Correction mode section at the top right of the Auto-Tune window. For the walk-throughs in this book, a mono vocal track works best in most cases.

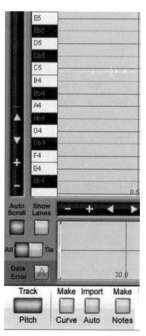

Now that Graphical mode housekeeping is out of the way, and you possess a thorough understanding of the Pitch Graph display, let's track some audio.

Track Pitch

Always initiate tracking on a silent part of the audio you wish to pitch correct. Starting on a portion of the file that contains audio data can cause the first moments of tracked audio to sound glitchy and therefore be difficult to pitch correct. If need be, create silence at the start of the project, or move the audio tracks in your project (together to keep sync) a few seconds to the right of 0 to accommodate this.

The Tracking knob's default setting of 50 works great nearly always, so let's leave it there.

With your DAW transport set to a suitable starting position, press Track Pitch in Auto-Tune. (Do not press Track Pitch + Time, which will be covered in depth in chapter 12.) Once pressed,

Figure 5.12

Figure 5.13

the Track Pitch button will begin flashing blue and red, indicating Auto-Tune is armed and ready for tracking.

Press Play on your DAW's transport to begin tracking audio into Graphical mode (most DAWs use the spacebar on the QWERTY keyboard for this action—this or the equivalent keyboard shortcut should be used, so you can visually monitor the tracking progress in Auto-Tune). As mentioned previously, it is recommended that you track in the entire file.

As your audio is tracked, a waveform will appear in the Pitch Graph display. When you are done tracking, hit Stop Playback on your DAW's transport. You should now see a series of thin, squiggly red lines across the waveforms of your tracked audio. If not, move the vertical scroll bar until they appear. With your cursor inside the Pitch Graph display, you can also use your mouse's vertical scroll wheel. These Red Curves (technically called Red Input Pitch Contour Data, or Red Curves for short) represent pitches in the tracked audio detected by Auto-Tune. If you zoom in on both axes of the Pitch Graph display, these Red Curves can easily be compared against the note lines or lanes stemming from the vertical axis. These Red Curves are for reference only. Not only do they provide a graphic representation of the high amount of pitch variations common to singing, they also show you how sharp or flat the vocal performance is on a note-by-note basis.

To play back audio tracked into Graphical mode, use your DAW's transport controls.

Where Auto mode shows you how flat or sharp an audio part is in real time via the Pitch Change Amount Meter, Graphical mode's Red Curves provide a static representation of the detected source pitches found in the source audio.

Zoom all the way in on both axes, scroll horizontally as needed, and take a few moments to study these Red Curves. This will take you far in gaining an understanding of the nature of pitch in vocals, and the pitch correction work before you. If your aim is a vocal effect, you will be straightening out these pitch changes and correcting them to exact notes. If your goal is transparent pitch correction, you will preserve these squiggles by degrees, while at the same time creating new ones on (or nearer to) the correct pitch. While that may sound like a daunting process, Auto-Tune makes it easy.

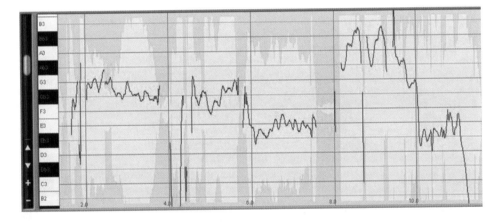

Figure 5.14

To get exact pitch information for these Red Curves down to 1 cent (1/100th of a semitone), place your cursor over them and look at the Detected Pitch display in the bottom-right corner of Graphical mode.

Figure 5.15

Graphical Mode Correction Objects

Before we can sensibly apply pitch correction to the audio you have just tracked into Graphical mode, we need to understand the myriad of tools available for pitch manipulation.

Graphical mode pitch correction relies on Correction objects being placed on the desired pitches, based on the Pitch Reference Lines or lanes inside the Pitch Graph display. As mentioned earlier, Auto-Tune offers three types of Correction objects. You can use any combination of these objects on any track, based on the audio's pitch correction needs.

Red Curves, Blue Curves, Green Curves

Auto-Tune's Graphical mode includes three different types of pitch contour data, commonly referred to as curves. Two of these are for reference purposes only; the third is an all-important Correction object that can be manipulated to adjust the amount of pitch correction applied.

- Red Curves (Red Input Pitch Contour Data)

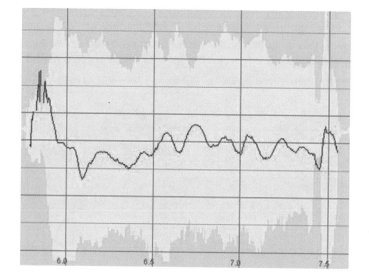

Figure 5.16

- As its formal name implies and as covered above, the Red Curves in the Pitch Graph display represent the original pitches found in audio tracked into Graphical mode. These are for reference only and cannot be manipulated. Without them, you cannot create the Correction objects required for pitch manipulation in Graphical mode. The number of Red Curves Auto-Tune creates can be influenced by the Tracking knob setting. At very relaxed Tracking knob settings, incidental noises—and even the vocalist's breath—can receive Red Input Pitch Curves. Red Curves on parts of the track that are not suitable for pitch correction (i.e., background noises and breathing sounds) should pose no problem, but in the unlikely event that they do, consider retracking the audio with a choosier Tracking setting. When Correction objects have been created over Red Curves Auto-Tune placed on incidental noises, you can safely ignore those objects, or select them and use the Cut button to remove them. For the walk-throughs in this book, leave tracking to its default of 50, and adjust only if Auto-Tune creates too few or too many Red Input Pitch Curves.

- Blue Curves (Blue Target Pitch Contour Objects)

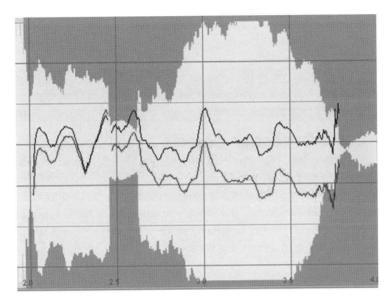

Figure 5.17. Blue Curves placed above Red Input Pitch Curves to correct flat notes.

- Blue Curves are Correction objects. They can be moved, stretched, squeezed and manipulated in order to adjust the pitches to which they relate. Of the three types of curves available in Graphical mode, Blue Curves are the only ones available for manipulation. The next section of this chapter explains in detail how and when to use these powerful Correction objects.
- Green Curves (Green Output Pitch Curves)

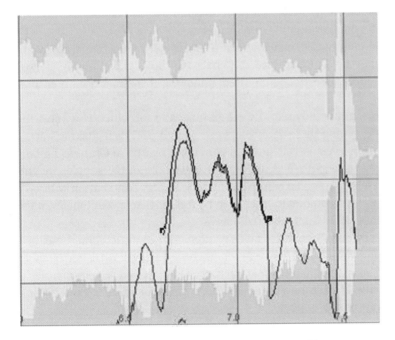

Figure 5.18. Green output curve just below its Blue Curve Correction object.

- Green Curves show the final output pitches based on your pitch correction editing. They are a by-product of Correction objects (including any Blue Curves present in the track), the per-object Retune Speeds assigned to them, and any per-object vibrato adjustments you have made. Blue Curves can sometimes be masked by Green Curves, depending on the Blue Curve's pitch correction settings. Since Green Curves can clutter the Pitch Graph display but are an important visual reference for final output pitch, assigning "Show Output Curves" to a key on your keyboard (via the Options menu) so they can easily be hidden or shown will benefit your workflow.

Creating Blue Curve Correction Objects

Blue Curve Correction objects offer a high level of manipulation and therefore are ideal for transparent, natural-sounding pitch correction. But that high level of control also means Curve objects, while far from difficult, are not necessarily the easiest to work with compared to other Correction objects. But since you can use the three types of Correction objects together, as you master Graphical mode pitch correction, you will become adept at identifying when to use curves versus when to use Correction Lines and Notes.

Blue Curves get created in one of three ways. They are created when you import Auto mode settings using the Import Auto button (this is covered in detail later in chapter 6). They are also created when you click the Make Curve button (located next to the Import Auto button beneath the Pitch Graph display). They can also be drawn in via the Curve tool, located in Graphical mode's Tools section just above the Pitch Graph display.

When using Auto-Tune's Import Auto feature, Blue Curves are created based on Key and Scale settings at the top of the Graphical mode window. When using the Make Curve button, Blue Curves are created on top of the Red Curves, and will therefore need to be moved manually to the correct notes for pitch correction to be applied. This is in large part what working in Graphical mode is

Figure 5.19

Figure 5.20

all about, and this level of control inside of Auto-Tune is key to discrete, transparent pitch correction. Not every Blue Curve needs to be moved, and when they are created in places where no pitch correction is required, removing them makes for a cleaner editing environment.

For performances that are only slightly out of tune, and for which you know the desired key and scale, setting these parameters accordingly and then clicking Import Auto is a very fast way to get excellent pitch correction results in Graphical mode. If intensive pitch correction is called for, or you are unsure of the song's key and scale, setting the scale to Chromatic before clicking the Import Auto button will force those Blue Curve Correction objects to be created no further than a semitone from the detected source pitches as shown by the Red Curves.

As you will soon see, all of Graphical mode's automatic Correction object creation methods (Import Auto, Make Curve, Make Notes, Make Notes from MIDI, and Number of Note Objects) can be applied to the whole track, or to just defined regions of audio.

In Chapter 6, you will learn how to apply these different methods of creating Correction Curves to your source audio.

Line Correction Objects

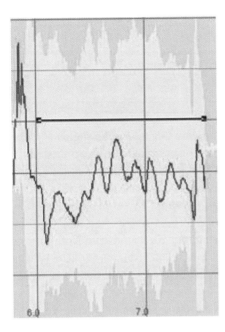

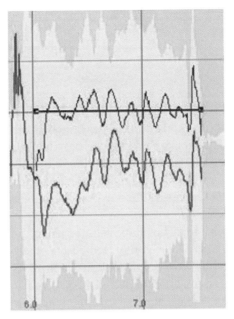

Figure 5.21. A Line Correction object placed on a Pitch Reference Line above a Red Input Pitch Curve.

Figure 5.22. The same Line Correction object accompanied by its Green Output Pitch Curve.

Line Correction objects cannot be created automatically like curves and notes. They must be drawn using the Line tool located in Graphical mode's Tools section above the Pitch Graph display.

Figure 5.23

Line Correction objects are excellent for both natural-sounding pitch correction and the Auto-Tune effect, and some find them easier to adjust and edit than Curve Correction objects.

As shown in chapter 6, Line objects can be segmented or cut into a series of short objects to deliver highly transparent pitch correction results, or to aid in the manipulation of melody.

Note Correction Objects

If Curve objects are precise and efficient (and they are), and Line objects are easy and effective (likewise true), Note objects are their brute-force counterparts. They are ideal for effect work, but can also be used transparently if the source audio only needs minor correction. Note objects accommodate a speedy workflow. They get created in four different ways—the Make Notes button, the Make Notes from MIDI button, the Note tool, and in conjunction with the I-Beam tool, the Number of Note Objects knob. Each is described below.

The Mighty Make Notes Button

Like the Make Curve button described above, the Make Notes button creates Note objects across all the audio tracked into Graphical mode (or a region of audio created using the I-Beam tool), based on the key and scale selected at the top of the Graphical mode window.

When working with Note objects, give the Show Lanes display mode a try. Lanes are an ideal reference for Note objects in most instances.

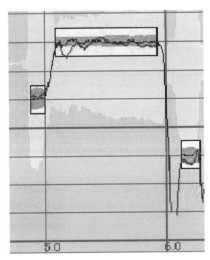

Figure 5.24

Figure 5.25

Number of Note Objects Knob

When you use the Make Notes button or use the I-Beam tool to select a region of audio in the Pitch Graph display, a previously grayed-out parameter in Graphical mode becomes available—Number of Note Objects. It is located below the Pitch Graph display and just to the right of the Make Notes button. As its name implies, this control defines how many Note objects are automatically created when clicking the Make Notes button.

With a region of audio selected using the I-Beam tool, the Number of Note Objects knob can also be used to create Note objects. Simply select a region with the I-Beam tool (or use it to double-click inside the Pitch Graph display to select the entire track), then click and turn the Note Objects knob.

Auto-Tune's automatic Note object creation function is more sensitive to pitch changes as you increase the Number of Note Objects setting, and less sensitive when you decrease it. For example, if the track you are working on includes vibrato, separate Note objects can get created for each change in pitch within that vibrato at high Number of Note Object settings. You probably do not want this. Remember, the Number of Note Objects knob remains grayed out unless you have already created Note objects, or unless you have selected audio inside of the Pitch Graph display using the I-Beam tool. Like many of Auto-Tune's settings, the default state of this parameter works great much of the time, and is a good place to start.

Nudging Objects

Located next to the Detected Pitch and Output Pitch displays near the bottom right of Graphical mode, you will find up and down Nudge buttons. Intuitive to use, these button allow you to nudge a selected Correction object (or objects) up or down from its current pitch location. Snap to Note must be turned off when nudging Note objects.

Figure 5.26

Each click of the up or down Nudge button moves the selected object 1 cent (1/100th of a semitone, or 1 pixel in the display). Humans rarely sing in perfect pitch, and nudging some objects just a few cents off of true pitch can help preserve an organic quality to the pitch correction process.

Graphical Mode Tools in Detail

Figure 5.27

Graphical mode offers a suite of tools to allow you to deftly move through your tracked audio and perform edits within the Pitch Graph display. Coupled with the Undo and

Redo buttons and other edit buttons, these tools allow you to experiment with, fine-tune, and manipulate pitch in countless ways. Many of these tools will be covered in detail within the walk-throughs that use them. Meanwhile, here is a list and brief description of the Graphical mode tools. Since our focus is still pitch correction and not time correction, this section does not cover the two-time tools, which are covered in depth in chapter 12.

Correction Object Drawing Tools

Each of Auto-Tune's three types of Correction objects has its own tool for drawing them in by hand inside the Pitch Graph display. Since you can only have one Correction object in a single location—though all three can be used across the track at your discretion—drawing a Correction object always replaces any existing Correction objects in the same time location. This makes it easy to try different Correction objects for specific parts of your track.

Figure 5.28

Line Tool

Line objects can only be created via the Line tool. This tool works in conjunction with Graphical mode's Snap to Note button. When Snap to Note is on, Line objects can only be drawn on note lines or lanes. If Scale is set to Major or Minor, then with Snap to Note on, Line objects can only be drawn on note lines that are a part of that scale. When Snap to Note is off, you can draw Line objects free-form.

Figure 5.29

Curve Tool

Drawing good Curve objects takes practice, and a great way to learn how to master the Curve tool is to study the curves Auto-Tune creates automatically. To draw a curve, simply select the Curve tool, move your cursor into the Pitch Graph display area, and start drawing. You can draw in any direction as long as you continue to hold down the mouse button. When you are ready to stop drawing, release the mouse button. Notice that when you've finished drawing, anchor points will appear at the curve's start and end points. These anchors can be moved using the Arrow tool, and thus any Blue Curve can be stretched, shrunk, or repositioned to cover more than one pitch at your discretion.

The Snap to Note feature does not affect the Curve tool, or Curve objects themselves.

Figure 5.30

Note Tool

Whether Snap to Note is on or off, Note objects are always drawn directly on exact pitches and therefore will always be drawn on the note reference line (or lane) closest to the Note tool cursor. However, with Snap to Note off, they can be nudged up or down in pitch via the Nudge buttons.

To draw Note objects with this tool, simply select it, then click, hold, and draw horizontally inside the Pitch Graph display.

Figure 5.31

Navigation and Object Editing Tools

The value of any editing environment is defined in large part by ease of navigation. Auto-Tune offers three tools to aid you in working inside of the Pitch Graph display.

Figure 5.32

Magnifying Glass

The Magnifying Glass tool takes the size of the area drawn with it and maximizes it within the Pitch Graph display. This tool is similar to the one found in the editing environment of most DAWs, and it behaves much the same way.

Figure 5.33

To use it, first select the tool, then click, hold, and drag around the area in the Pitch Graph display that you want to focus and zoom in on. Since it works on both horizontal and vertical axes, it may not always provide maximum zoom.

Its default state will show a plus sign inside the "glass" of the tool. When this is displayed, single-clicking inside the Pitch Graph display with this tool will zoom in one step (if not already at maximum zoom) while centering the clicked point inside the Pitch Graph display window. Holding down the Control key (Windows) or Option key (Mac) will change the aforementioned plus to a minus, at which point a single-click zooms out one step.

The Magnifying Glass also works in the Envelope Graph display. Use it here to select a region to be displayed in the Pitch Graph display. In fact, when using any other tool except the I-Beam tool, moving your cursor down into the Envelope Graph display will cause the cursor to change into the Magnifying Glass tool for navigational purposes. To select a region of audio in the Envelope Graph display to be shown in the Pitch Graph display, simply click, hold, and drag the magnifying glass horizontally.

I-Beam Tool

The I-Beam tool is a navigation tool and a selection tool. In the Pitch Graph display, use it to highlight a section of audio where you wish to import Auto mode settings or place Curve objects or Note objects using their respective buttons.

Figure 5.34

If you already have Correction objects inside the Pitch Graph display, you can use the I-Beam tool to edit groups of Correction objects en masse.

Double-clicking anywhere in the Pitch Graph display with the I-Beam tool will select all of the audio tracked into Graphical mode. Using this tool in the Envelope Graph display allows you to create a region of audio anywhere on the track and have it appear in the Pitch Graph display. If the region created this way was not previously visible in the Pitch Graph display, it will be once the region has been defined.

To use this tool, select it; then click, hold, and drag horizontally.

Hand Tool

Use the Hand tool to manually move what is shown in the Pitch Graph display. When you use it to move horizontally, it moves the audio viewable in the Pitch Graph display forward or backward. When you use it to move vertically, it moves the note lines (or lanes) on the vertical axis.

Figure 5.35

Arrow Tool

The Arrow tool serves multiple editing functions:

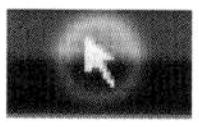

Figure 5.36

- **Selection:** You can use the Arrow tool to select individual or multiple Correction objects for moving, or for adjusting object-specific parameters such as per-object Retune Speed. To do this, click on a single Correction object in between its ends or anchor points; or to select multiple Correction objects, click and drag a section of tracked audio in the Pitch Graph display, similar to how you use the I-Beam tool. When selecting multiple Correction objects with the Arrow tool, you must, however, click and drag outside of any Correction objects, since clicking on them with this tool opens up more editing functions.

- **Moving Objects:** Use the Arrow tool to move Correction objects either vertically (pitch) or horizontally (time) while preserving the contour of the object being moved. You must hold down Control (Windows) or Option (Mac) to move objects horizontally, at which point the Arrow tool cursor will change to a four-arrow cursor (for Note objects) or crosshairs (for lines and curves). If you have selected a region of tracked audio with either the Arrow tool or the I-Beam tool, then all Correction objects within that selected region will be moved. While new Correction objects can be drawn over existing Correction objects, causing them to be replaced with the newly drawn object, this behavior does not apply when moving Correction objects. In other words, horizontal movement is constrained by adjacent Correction objects.

- **Editing Length and Contour of Correction Lines and Curves:** Click on a Correction Line or Curve's end or anchor point to move that point vertically or horizontally (again, you must use the above-mentioned key modifiers for horizontal movements), thereby changing the contour or length (or both) of Curve and Line objects. For Line objects, which can contain anchor points within the line itself, you can also use the Arrow tool to click those anchor points and thus move a line segment either vertically or horizontally as described above. When editing Correction Lines and Curves in this way, Auto-Tune gives you the freedom to dramatically change their shape or contour. Freedom is power, and since undo is a quick click away, this is a great place to experiment when using different Correction object shapes for transparent pitch correction, pitch effects, melody work, and applying pitch correction to highly stylized performances. Because the contour of Curve objects is initially defined by Red Input Curves, moving Blue Curves in time rarely achieves positive results. Line and Note objects, however, are much friendlier when it comes to moving them in time. Similar to moving entire objects horizontally, extending the length of Line and Curve objects is constrained by existing objects.
- **Adding or Deleting Anchor Points:** Double-clicking with the Arrow tool on a portion of a Line object will add an anchor point at the click point, which can then be moved as described above. Double-clicking on top of an existing anchor point will delete it from the Line object. Of course, end anchor points cannot be deleted.
- **Changing the Length of Note Objects:** If you click and hold the start or end of a Note object with the Arrow tool, you can then drag it horizontally to shorten or lengthen the Note object without employing a modifier key on your computer keyboard. If you drag it to an area that includes other Correction objects, those objects will be replaced by the Note object you are extending. Note objects are the only Correction objects that, when extended via the Arrow tool, will replace adjacent objects. In chapter 10, "Mastering the Auto-Tune Vocal Effect," you will see how you can use this to streamline effect creation in Graphical mode.

In the next chapter, you will put these editing techniques to work.

Scissors Tool

Use this tool to cut Correction objects into smaller objects. This can be put to good use with Note objects when creating the Auto-Tune effect, and for assigning different Retune Speed amounts for parts that previously contained a single Correction object. Using the Scissors tool to cut long Blue Curves into smaller ones allows for more surgical pitch editing, and is quite effective when pitch correcting long notes and passages.

Figure 5.37

Correction objects created using the Scissors tool will retain the per-object parameters of the object from which they were cut.

Graphical Mode Edit Buttons

No editing environment would be complete without copy, cut, and paste functionality. Auto-Tune's Graphical mode offers these as buttons located to the right of Graphical mode's Tools section above the Pitch Graph display. Their button names

Figure 5.38

convey exactly what they do, and their behaviors are the same as similarly named functions in your DAW, your word processor, and your computer.

The only exception worth noting here is the Clear All button, located to the far left of Graphical mode's tools section. Clicking this button removes everything, including tracked audio from the Pitch Graph display. This function cannot be undone, and a dialog box will appear to remind you of this. You can suppress the appearance of this dialog box by holding down the Shift key while clicking Clear All.

Selecting Correction Objects for Editing

There are three ways to select Correction objects for copying, cutting, and pasting. They are:

- **Select All Button:** Clicking this button selects all Correction objects in the tracked audio, which you can then copy or cut.
- **I-Beam Tool:** Remember, this tool is for defining a region of audio for editing. When creating a region with this tool, any Correction objects within that region can be copied or cut to the Auto-Tune clipboard for pasting in a different location inside the Pitch Graph display.
- **Arrow Tool:** Use this tool to select a single Correction object by clicking on it, or click, hold, and drag inside the Pitch Graph display to select a group of objects.

To paste copied or cut Correction objects, simply click on the Paste button, and then click and hold somewhere in the Pitch Graph display. When you perform this click and hold, you will see the Correction objects you are about to paste. You can move this block of data around the Pitch Graph display until you are satisfied with the location, and then release the click to initiate the paste. Give it a try, it's quite easy to do.

Graphical Mode as a Pitch Analyzer

You've already le arned how Auto mode's tools and interface can be used for analysis purposes. Graphical mode simplifies pitch analysis by providing a readout of detected pitches, Correction object pitches, and final output pitches.

Object Pitch Display

Located beneath the right-hand corner of the Pitch Graph display, the Object Pitch display shows the pitch of any Correction object in the same time location as the cursor. Since each Correction object can have its own Retune Speed and vibrato settings, object pitch may not always match the output pitch at the same location.

Output Pitch Display

Located in the bottom-right corner of the Graphical mode window, Output Pitch display shows the actual output pitch at the current cursor location. This display reflects the output pitches revealed by the Green Output Curves whether they are present or not.

Detected Pitch Display

Hover your cursor over any part of the audio waveform shown in the Pitch Graph display, and the Detected Pitch display will show you what pitch Auto-Tune has detected at that cursor location. Red Curves must be present in the same time location as your cursor. This is a great way to learn the key and scale of your audio when it is not obvious. It also reveals just how far off the performance is, which can help you determine your pitch correction needs. The Detected Pitch display is located in the bottom-right corner of the Graphical mode window.

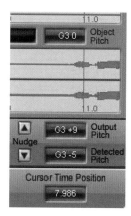

Figure 5.39

Cursor Time Position Display

All this pitch information at your fingertips would be meaningless without a reference as to where in the tracked audio (and therefore where in your project) you are. The Cursor Time Position display, located beneath the Detected Pitch display, provides this information. Assuming your DAW sends valid project clock information to Auto-Tune, this window should also match your project time. Values in this display will be either bars and beats or seconds, depending on the Time display you have selected.

Chapter **6**

MASTERING PITCH CORRECTION IN GRAPHICAL MODE

In chapter 5, you learned about all the tools and features available in Auto-Tune's Graphical mode, and how to set up this mode for an ideal pitch correction editing environment. Now let's experience the power of Graphical mode pitch correction editing.

This chapter assumes you have a vocal recording tracked into Graphical mode, as explained in chapter 5. If not, track audio as described in the previous chapter before continuing.

You should know by now how to identify your audio's pitch correction needs through listening and looking at those Red Input Curves. It's now time to start applying pitch correction through the cunning use of Correction objects.

Correcting with Curves

No doubt about it, Graphical mode is complex; Graphical mode is deep; Graphical mode is surgically precise. It can also be exceedingly easy to use.

As covered previously in this book, Curve objects are extremely powerful Correction objects, especially when your goal is transparent pitch correction. Thanks to the Import Auto button, they can also be easy to use.

Correction Curves with a Single Click

The goal of this walk-through is professional, transparent pitch correction. In other words, pitch correction as a tool and not as an effect (Auto-Tune for effect purposes is covered in depth in chapter 10).

1. With your audio tracked into Graphical mode, set Key and Scale at the top of the Graphical mode window if you know it. If not, set the Scale to Chromatic. Click over to Auto mode and set Retune Speed to 20 (the default), and make sure all other settings except Key and Scale are turned off or set to their null states. Go ahead and play back the audio until you are familiar with how it sounds processed with these current Auto mode settings.

2. Back in Graphical mode, adjust the Pitch Graph display so you can see all of the tracked audio as well as the Red Input Curves. Do not have Auto-Tune show Green Output Curves at this time. (You should already have this feature set to toggle on and off via a key on your QWERTY keyboard.)

3. Click on the Import Auto button. Since you did not select a region for editing via the I-Beam tool, Blue Correction Curves will be placed across the entire track, based on the selected key and scale and the location of the Red Curves. Depending on those parameters and how far out of tune the source audio is, these Blue Curves may be close to or even on top of the Red Input Pitch Curves.

4. If you know the vocal track's key and scale and have set it appropriately in Auto-Tune prior to clicking the Make Curve button, then you are largely done. Play back the audio and hear the results, basking in the speed at which you applied professional transparent pitch correction in Graphical mode. Do not be surprised, however, if in your desire for highly professional results, you need to fine-tune the Retune Speed or placement of a few individual curves. This will be especially true on longer notes, vibrato passages, and other sections containing highly stylistic performances. These are the kind of edits Graphical mode is designed to accommodate.

   Play back the audio a few times (both solo and against the music in your project) in order to really get a sense of what Auto-Tune and those Blue Correction Curves are doing, and which curves need fine-tuning or removal outright. It should sound identical to Auto mode playback in step 1 assuming the Default Retune Speed matches what you set in Auto Mode. Keep in mind that Formant button, and if any Blue Curves are more than a semitone away from their corresponding Red Curves, Formant should be switched on to keep broad changes in pitch sounding natural.

   Remember, Graphical mode is designed to pitch correct notes and sections of audio independently, and using Auto-Tune as a tool and not an effect includes applying pitch correction only where needed, and manipulating placement, shape and per-object settings of individual Correction objects.

5. Select the Arrow tool, and use it to move Blue Curves as needed to perfect the application of transparent pitch correction. Keep in mind that when you use the Import Auto button, Graphical mode treats those curves as if they have all been selected (same goes for Make Curve and Make Notes buttons). So before you can select a specific curve for editing, first click in an area inside the Pitch Graph display where no curves exist. This deselects all curves, so you can then click and select individual ones.

   In some cases, you may want to shift up or down in pitch just the start or end points on some of the newly created Blue Curves, to allow subtle amounts of pitch nuances of the performance to come through, and to keep the pitch correction process discrete and not heavy-handed. As you grow intimately familiar with the vocalists you work with and the tracks you are pitch correcting, there is a very good chance you will find patterns to their pitchiness. Some singers are only pitchy near the ends of notes, others at the beginning, and some may be uniformly flat or sharp. Use this knowledge to edit Correction objects in a way that corrects pitch problems while respecting the performance.

   Before editing long curves over vibrato parts and long notes, use the Scissors tool to cut them into smaller Correction objects more malleable for manipulation. This gives you a high degree of control over long notes and passages. Fine-tuning the placement of these newly created smaller curves, decreasing their Retune Speeds, or even removing these curves altogether can help meet the surgically precise and highly transparent pitch correction needs of vibratos and other highly stylized passages.

   It is rare that pitch correction work requires moving Curve objects horizontally in time. This can cause bad results, since these curves were created based on the subtle pitch changes Auto-Tune detected and captured as Red Curve data in your tracked audio. If you need to adjust the horizontal placement of pitch correction objects, try using Line objects or Note objects. Again, keep in mind that a well-performed vibrato part may be best served by either having no Correction object over it or one with a slow Retune Speed. Cutting up a curve and removing just the curve over the attack portion of a note or passage can also be effective. Same goes for decreasing Retune Speed on long notes, vibrato parts, and eloquent passages where you want emotion, perhaps even vulnerability, to rule over pitch precision. You can also stretch a curve over a vibrato that is a bit wild in order to tame it. After a few edits, you should find this a very intuitive process. Remember to use undo and redo to A/B your edits as needed.

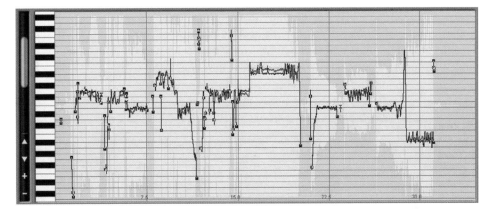

Figure 6.1. Blue Curves created using the Import Auto function. The smaller, highly vertical curves are on noises in the track that do not require pitch correction and should be removed. The longer curves may need to be cut into smaller curves for more precise editing.

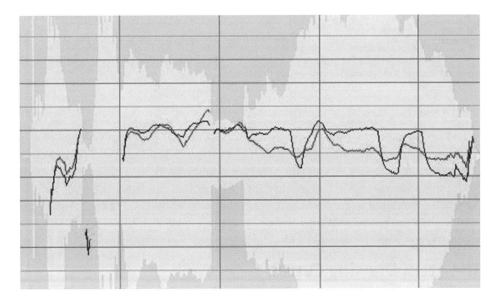

Figure 6.2. A zoomed-in view of Blue Curves created using the Import Auto function.

Using the Make Curve Button

Try the above walk-through again, only instead of using the Import Auto button, use the Make Curve button. Doing so will create Blue Curves right on top of Red Curves. In other words, all the necessary curves will be created, but until you move them to the desired pitches, no pitch correction will be applied, though all those Blue Curves will be available for per-object parameter editing (Retune Speed, Adjust Vibrato, and Throat Length Adjust).

This is a common Graphical mode workflow. It creates all the elements required for precise and highly transparent pitch correction. The next step is editing—moving each curve to the correct pitch as needed along with adjusting their contours, changing any per-object settings, cutting large curves into a series of smaller ones as needed for more precise manipulation, and removing curves that are not needed. While this may sound like a lot of work, it can be a straightforward and fairly quick process once you understand the pitch correction requirements of the track. This is, after all, the kind of work Graphical mode is designed to accommodate. And know that this is the kind of pitch correction treatment many professional singers receive, and every great singer deserves. For the sake of workflow, it's always worth trying Import Auto first. This delivers the same numbers of curves, only they are placed at pitches set by Auto mode's parameters. In other words, the Make Curve and Import Auto buttons are both great starting points for surgical pitch editing in Graphical mode.

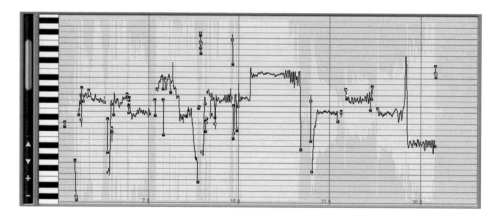

Figure 6.3. Tracked audio with curves created using the Make Curve button.

Once you are satisfied with your edits, whether you render or mix down the track to make it permanent is largely a question of workflow. If you do, it's a good idea to create a backup of the audio track first. If your DAW is sending valid project clock information to Auto-Tune, you can close the plug-in window, and Graphical mode pitch correction will still be applied. In the rare event that this is not the case, you will have little choice but to render or mix down the track or the project with Auto-Tune open. If your project or DAW suffers from resource issues, then likewise, rendering or mixing down the pitch-corrected audio can help resource management.

The Art of Drawing Curves

Figure 6.4

As you just experienced, working with curves can be a fast and effective means for surgical pitch correction editing. Drawing curves, however, takes a bit more practice to perfect. Yet Graphical mode would be incomplete without this feature.

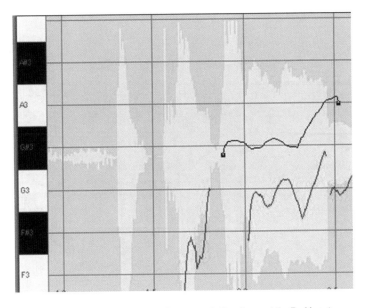

Figure 6.5. Curve drawn over a note that respects the shape of the Red Input
Pitch Curve while changing pitch to higher notes.

When drawing curves, try zooming in to the maximum level on the vertical axis (the horizontal axis should be zoomed to accommodate viewing the section of audio you are drawing a curve over). At this level, 1 pixel in the Pitch Graph display equals 1 cent of pitch change (Remember: 100 cents = 1 semitone, or 1 half-step). This makes it much easier to draw curves that are natural sounding and contain the small degrees of pitch change common to singing, as detected by Auto-Tune and shown via the Red Curves. Conversely, you may find that zooming out vertically to around the halfway point is ideal when using the Curve tool for melody work.

To draw a curve, simply select the Curve tool, click and hold inside the Pitch Graph display at the point you wish the curve to begin, then start drawing. Release the click at the point at which you wish the curve to end. Once you have drawn the curve, you can use the Arrow tool to move it or change its contour, or move its start or end point to different pitches to create glissandos.

Drawing curves can be aided greatly by using the Red Input Pitch Curves as a reference.

Just because the tool is called a Curve tool does not mean you must draw curves with it. Its free-form ability allows for the drawing of any shape, including a straight line.

Reasons for Breaking out the Curve Tool

- **Manually Drawing in Vibrato:** Even with Auto-Tune's comprehensive suite of vibrato creation controls, some people prefer to create their own signature vibrato by drawing it in via the Curve tool. It's easy to do, hard to master, and comes at the expense of amplitude and formant variations that occur naturally in vibrato performances and that are available in Auto mode's Create Vibrato section. The benefits are that it offers unprecedented control over the width and speed of the vibrato as it unfolds. And remember, human vibrato width and speed are almost never static.

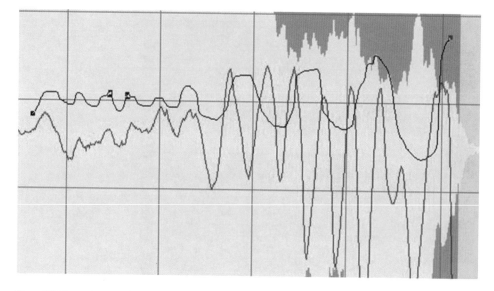

Figure 6.6. Curve drawn to change vibrato shape and put in pitch.

- **Humanization:** Mastering Auto-Tune includes making the pitch-corrected audio sound as natural and unprocessed-sounding as possible. For transparent pitch correction, the vocal track should just sound in tune and not effected. In most cases, this can be attained by fine-tuning pitch correction parameters on a per-object basis. But in other cases, often as the result of a badly out-of-tune performance, extra steps must be taken to humanize and demechanize applied pitch correction. The Curve tool can come to the rescue here if used judiciously. Often the need for humanization pertains to elongated notes that sound overly static due to the amount of pitch correction required to make them in tune. On these long notes, drawing in curves can bring back the organic quality of the human voice. A little goes a very long way here, and typical to the Curve tool, this will take some practice to master. The need for such editing should also be a rare event. If this becomes a normal part of your workflow, than either you need to better master your use of pitch correction parameters, including those shared between Auto mode and Graphical mode, or you need to spend more time during the recording process in order to capture performances that do not require heavy-handed use of pitch correction. And if the singer simply cannot pull off a relatively in-tune performance—well, you are in good company, and purchasing this book was a wise decision.

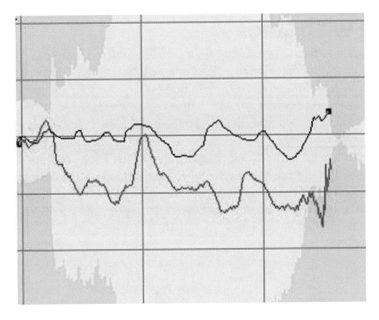

Figure 6.7. Curve drawn on pitch with rhythmic nuances preserved for transparent pitch correction.

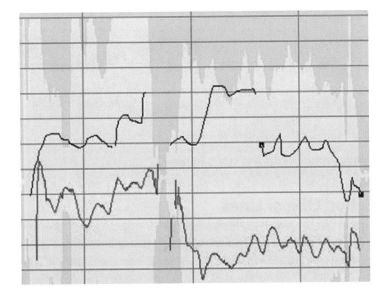

Figure 6.8. Curves drawn to change melody.

- **Melody Creation:** Auto-Tune has been put to good use as a tool for recreating and editing melody. The popular "Auto-Tune the News" series by the Gregory Brothers probably would not exist without this ability. The Curve tool lets you easily recreate melodies by simply drawing them in (though as you'll soon see, the Line and Note tools often deliver better results). It takes a steady hand and some trial and error, but it's not that difficult. The trick here is to use curves that are short in duration, and switch on Auto-Tune's Formant control so notes a few semitones away from the original pitch will sound natural. This will be covered in greater detail in chapter 10, "Mastering the Auto-Tune Vocal Effect."

Figure 6.9

Correcting with Lines

The Line tool is designed to facilitate drawing segmented lines across one or more pitches. These cannot be created automatically like Curve and Note objects, and must be drawn using the Line tool, located in Graphical mode's Tools section above the Pitch Graph display. Line objects are easier to draw than Curve objects, since you can conform them to only be drawn on specific pitches of the selected scale, using the Snap to Note feature. As you will see when you bring in the Green Output Pitch Curves, using a Line object does not mean that you are flattening out the pitch contours of the performance. Those contours remain intact when working with Line objects, depending on your per-object parameter settings.

With the Snap to Note function engaged, Line objects are a powerful way to use Auto-Tune for melody manipulation.

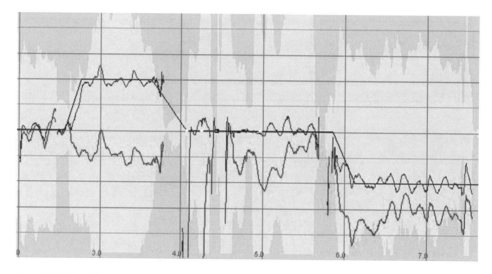

Figure 6.10. Line objects drawn on a minor scale with Snap to Note on. Notice Green Output Curves show that subtle pitch changes are preserved.

Drawing Correction Object Lines

Snap to Note is on by default in Graphical mode. Since it is well suited for line drawing, let's leave it on as we walk through using the Line tool. If you still have Blue Curves from the Curve object walk-through, use the Undo button to remove them (click it until you only have Red Input Pitch Curves), or use the Clear All button to clear everything in the Pitch Graph display. (Using Clear All means you will have to track audio again).

For this walk-through, first hide the Green Pitch Output Curves. Next, find a small portion (5 to 10 seconds is plenty) of out-of-tune audio (ideally a half-step off or less) and make sure you are zoomed in on it inside the Pitch Graph display. Also make sure you can see the Red Curves. Show Lanes should be off.

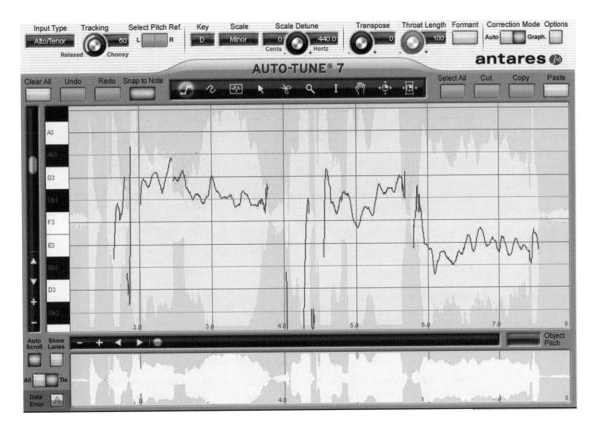

Figure 6.11

The goal of this walk-through is to create a multisegmented Line object that alters melody. This is quite suitable when working with the Auto-Tune effect.

1. With your audio tracked into Graphical mode, set the Key and Scale at the top of the Graphical mode window if you know it. If not, set Scale to Chromatic.

2. Select the Line tool by clicking on it in the Tools section. Using the Red Curve data and the waveform as pitch and location references, begin drawing your Line object by single-clicking on the Pitch Reference Line closest to the Red Curve of the note or section you will be pitch correcting. If you are unsure if the section you are correcting is flat or sharp, and therefore unsure where to draw your Line object, just pick one, and if it's not right, use the power of undo.

3. Extend the line to cover the portion of audio selected for pitch correction in this walk-through. When you have reached the point where you want the line to end, double-click. The line you have just drawn will be shown in the display as a dark blue line resting exactly on top of the gray note line (Pitch Reference Line).

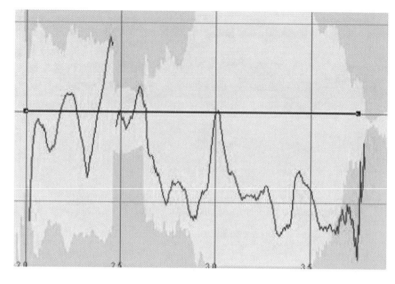

Figure 6.12

4. Show the Green Output Pitch Curve so you can visualize the results. Notice that the Green Curve largely matches the contour of its associated Red Curve, and any variance here is largely due to that Line object's Retune Speed. Also notice that the Green Curve will be largely centered on the pitch line where you drew your Line object.

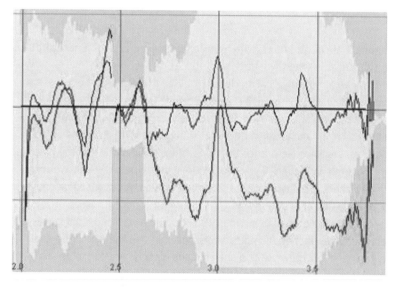

Figure 6.13

5. Press Play on your DAW to hear the results. Use undo and redo so you can play back the audio pre- and post-pitch correction. Doing this is a great way to monitor transparent pitch correction processing.

Congratulations, you have just surgically applied pitch correction to a small portion of your audio track. And by doing so, you have unlocked the power of Auto-Tune as found in your record collection and used on a daily basis by professional engineers and artists around the world.

Now let's draw a segmented line so you can explore Auto-Tune's melody-creation capabilities.

First, click the Undo button to remove the line you have just drawn, as described in the previous paragraph.

1. Again, select the Line tool if it is not already selected, and make sure Snap to Note is on and the Green Curves are hidden. This time you may want to zoom out on the vertical axis, so you can clearly see at least two note lines that are part of the current scale.

2. Click on the note line (as described above) where you want to start drawing your Line object. Extend the line to about the halfway point of the section of audio you are pitch correcting.

3. Now single-click again, and move the Line tool up or down to the next full-step note line in the current scale. Once again, the choice of whether this is above or below the note where you began drawing is up to you, and if you don't like the result, undo to the rescue. If you want a dramatic shift between the two notes used in this exercise (think Auto-Tune effect), the portion of the line between the two notes should be perfectly vertical. For a more natural effect, the portion of the line between notes should be drawn at an angle. Don't focus too much on this line angle, as you will soon learn how you can go back and change it.

4. Now, with the Line tool on the second note line of this drawing exercise, single-click again, then continue extending the line to the right until you reach the end of the section you are pitch correcting.

5. Double-click to stop drawing the line. You should now see a segmented line that is somewhat Z-shaped or reverse-Z-shaped, depending on whether you ended on a note higher or lower than the starting note. Sonically you have taken the section you are pitch correcting and given it a two-note melody. You could have just as easily drawn the line over a section of audio that starts on one note and finishes on another using the same notes (or intended notes) as shown by the Red Curves. In this case, you would not be creating a new melody, but rather applying pitch correction (either as an effect or with transparency based on this object's Retune Speed) in a way that preserves the existing melody.

   If your Line object was drawn across pitches more than a semitone apart, you should turn on Auto-Tune's Formant feature, since it is designed to establish natural-sounding formants on audio that has been corrected well above or below its original pitch. Without it, large changes in pitch applied by Auto-Tune would sound unnatural. This is a good time to understand the importance of this parameter. Play back your audio with the Formant button turned on and turned off. The further away the corrected pitch is from the original detected pitch, the more important this parameter becomes, and the more unnatural the formant characteristics will be when it's turned off. The closer the corrected notes are to the original pitches, the less noticeable formant changes will be. So much so that the Formant button could be left off. However, when doing melody work or making large changes in pitch, the Formant button should always be on. Without this parameter, Auto-Tune's ability to recreate melody would not sound authentic.

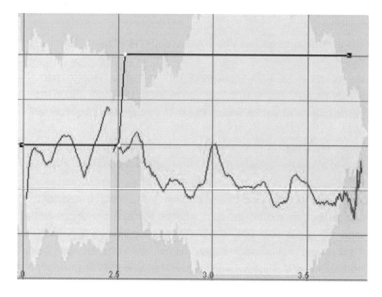

Figure 6.14

6. Press play on your DAW to hear the results. Again, use undo and redo to compare the audio pre– and post–pitch correction.

7. Lastly, apply different per-object Retune Speeds to the entire Line object created in this walk-through. To do this, use the Arrow tool or I-Beam tool and create a region that includes the entire Line object, thus selecting it. Use the per-object Retune Speed knob below the Pitch Graph display, and play back the audio at different Retune Speed amounts, including 0, the fastest setting (hello, Auto-Tune effect); and 400, the slowest setting. Notice that at fast Retune Speed amounts, the melody work will be quite obvious, and the Auto-Tune effect will be heard. At slower Retune Speeds, this Line object's impact on melody will be more subtle.

Every time you single-click with the Line tool while drawing, you create an anchor point that locks the line between it and the previous point. When you double-click with the Line tool, you end the line, leaving behind a final anchor point that can still be manipulated.

Even though this walk-through had you draw lines to the right, moving you forward in the project, you could just as easily have started at the right of the section and drawn the line object to the left.

This is just one example of the power of Auto-Tune for melody and pitch manipulation. Now let's experiment with manipulating the Line objects you have just drawn.

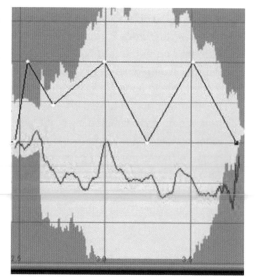

Figure 6.15

Editing and Moving Line Objects with the Arrow Tool

The Arrow tool can manipulate a Line object in three different ways. It can move an entire Line object or one of its segments up or down in pitch (or horizontally in time if Control [Windows] or Option [Mac] is held down). It can be used to change the shape of the Line object by clicking and dragging an anchor point to a new location. And it can be used to add or delete anchor points from an existing Line object.

When selecting a Line object with the Arrow tool, if the line contains multiple segments, then clicking it with the Arrow tool only selects the segment where it was clicked. That segment can then be moved and manipulated as described below. To select an entire Line object with the Arrow tool, create a region with the tool that includes the entire object.

Select the Arrow tool from the Tools section, and use it to select the entire line you have just drawn. Once the Line object has been selected, you will see a series of anchor points where you single- and double-clicked during the line-drawing process (if the Line object was already selected, then these anchor points were already visible). These are the anchor points covered in chapter 5, and they mark the segment boundaries of any Line Correction object, whether it has one segment (a single line), or multiple segments, such as the Z-shaped line you just drew.

To move the entire Line object, place the Arrow tool over a section of the selected line that does not have an anchor point. The Arrow tool cursor should now appear as two arrows, one up, one down. Click and hold on the line with this cursor, and you'll be able to move it up or down to a different pitch. Again, if you hold down Control (Windows) or Option (Mac) while clicking, the Arrow tool cursor will change to a horizontal line, and you can move the Line object horizontally in time. Remember, adjacent Correction objects will constrain horizontal movements.

To edit the shape of a Line object, place the Arrow tool cursor over an anchor point, and then click, hold, and move that anchor to a new location (the same Windows and Mac modifier keys apply for horizontal movements). To move an entire segment, click on the segment in between anchor points to select just that segment. Use these methods to change the shape of the Line object you just drew in order to understand how changing the shape of a Line object can affect pitch and melody work.

You can also select a line with the Arrow tool and then use the Nudge buttons to nudge the line up or down in pitch. Nudging lines works whether Snap to Note is on or off.

Adding or Removing Anchor Points

Double-clicking with the Arrow tool anywhere on a Line object that does not have an anchor point will create one.

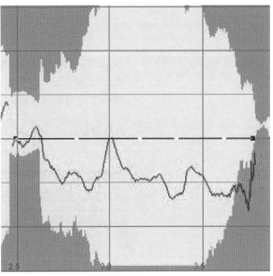

Figure 6.16

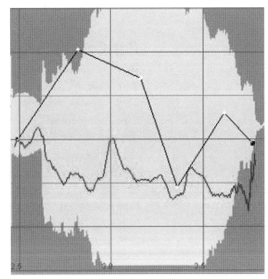

Figure 6.17. The same line shown in Figure 6.16 with its anchor points moved to different pitches.

Try it. Double-clicking on an existing anchor point with the Arrow tool will delete it. You cannot delete anchor points that start or end a Line object. Now is a good time to try this as well.

For some, double-clicking to terminate a line feels "sticky," as if the cursor refuses to let go of the line. The reason for this lies in how the Line tool double-click is employed. If you single-click, draw your line, then single-click again, you've set an anchor point and created a segment as described above. If instead you want to end the line, you need only click once more, provided you are on the same reference pitch line as the previous click.

When double-clicking with the Line tool, the time between clicks does not matter; only the cursor position does. Pressing the Escape key on your QWERTY keyboard will also terminate the line.

Lastly, holding down the Control key (Windows) or Option key (Mac) will force the Line tool to draw only horizontally, assuming your DAW surrenders control of this key when working in Auto-Tune.

Experimenting with Per-Object Parameters

As revealed in step 7 in the above walk-through, when a Correction object (or objects) is selected, a previously grayed-out section of Graphical mode becomes available. This section, just above Graphical mode's Clock section, is where you set, on a Correction-object basis, Retune Speed, Throat Length Adjust, and vibrato width (Adjust Vibrato).

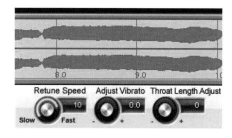

Figure 6.18

Per-Object Retune Speed

In order to understand how final pitch output is shaped by both Correction objects and these aforementioned object-specific parameters, especially Retune Speed, bring

back the Green Curves, and with the Line object still selected, adjust the per-object Retune Speed (not the global Retune Speed at the top of the Graphical and Auto mode windows) to its slowest speed (400 milliseconds) and watch what happens to that Green Curve.

Notice that as Retune Speed is decreased for the Line object you have drawn, the Green Output Pitch Curve will move closer in location to the Red Input Pitch Curve, and mirror its contour even more. This is illustrated in Figure 6.19.

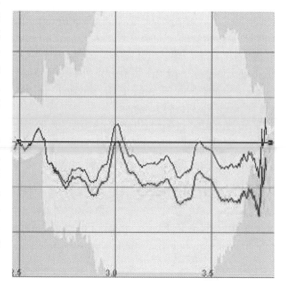

Figure 6.19

With the Line object still selected, set the Retune Speed knob to 0, its fastest setting, and watch that Green Curve. At a Retune Speed of 0, which we now know is the right setting for attaining the Auto-Tune effect, the Green Output Pitch Curve will become a straight line and be in the identical position as the Line object you have drawn. This makes sense, since a 0 Retune Speed flattens out the nuances of natural singing, which is in large part how the Auto-Tune effect gets created. Watching the Green Curve change as you adjust per-object Retune Speed is a great way to visualize how Retune Speed affects pitch correction transparency (or the lack of).

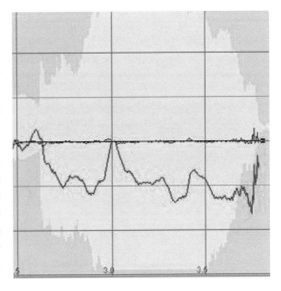

Figure 6.20. With the per-object Retune Speed knob set to 3, the Green Output Pitch Curve is almost perfectly flat.

While we're at it, let's go ahead and tweak the Adjust Vibrato and Throat Length parameters for the same Line object.

Per-Object Adjust Vibrato

The per-object Adjust Vibrato parameter is designed to increase or decrease the width of a vibrato present in the source audio that has a Correction object applied to it. In other words, adjusting this parameter can help Auto-Tune apply appropriate levels of pitch correction while preserving vibrato captured in the performance. This is a trial-and-error kind of parameter. If dialing in this parameter does not help manage pitch correction over a vibrato section, then look to the Draw Curve tool for additional help, or Auto mode's more comprehensive vibrato controls, which once set can be imported into Graph via the Import Auto function. To see its sometimes dramatic effect on output pitch as shown by Green Curves, set the object's Retune Speed to 0, and then turn this knob clockwise and counterclockwise. Also look at chapter 8, which is dedicated to vibrato management in Auto-Tune.

Per-Object Throat Length Adjust

The last Correction-object-specific parameter to cover is Throat Length Adjust. Even with the Line object selected, this parameter will remain grayed out until you click on the Formant button at the top of the Graphical mode window. With Formant engaged, both of Graphical mode's Throat Length Adjust knobs will become available for use. The one at the top is global and also applies to Auto mode. The one beneath the Pitch Graph display is, like its Retune Speed and Adjust Vibrato neighbors, object specific. Once again, select the Line object you have created, click on the Formant button, and turn the Throat Length Adjust knob while watching the Green Output Pitch Curve. Notice what happens to the Green Curve—nothing! As discussed in chapter 4, Throat Length parameters are independent of the pitch correction process. Play back the corrected section of audio while adjusting this parameter, and you will see that it can be put to good use as an effect.

Line Object Segments and Per-Object Parameters

Segments created when drawing lines can have their own per-object parameters, such as Retune Speed, making Line objects fast and flexible to work with. Just use the Arrow tool to click on a segment, thereby making it available for per-object parameter adjustments.

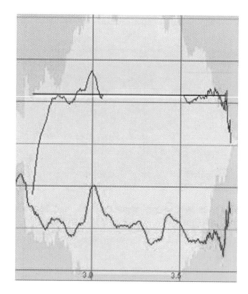

Figure 6.21. A multisegment Line object with the middle segment's Retune Speed set to 0.

The next section describes how to apply the same flexibility to Curve and Note objects.

The Scissor Tool and Per-Object Parameters

Curve and Note objects can sometimes be large objects to work with. Unlike Line objects, curves and notes cannot be segmented, so their per-object parameters cover the entire Curve or Note object regardless of how large or small they are. Large Curve and Note objects can be less than ideal for performing surgically precise pitch edits. The solution here is a simple one—the Scissors tool.

Use the Scissors tool to cut large Curve and Note objects into smaller ones that can each receive its own per-object parameters. When a single Curve object has been created across notes containing vibrato, this is often a requirement, since it allows different Retune Speeds for the early part of the note and the part containing vibrato, which, as you should know by now, likely needs a slower Retune Speed setting.

When using the Scissors tool for this kind of editing, the rhythm of the performance and the beats of the song, as well as melody and how far corrected pitches are from the source pitch, are all factors in deciding where to make these cuts.

Objects created with the Scissors tool will keep the same per-object settings that were applied to the object from which they were cut.

The Scissors tool aids workflow by allowing you to divide larger Correction objects into smaller ones while preserving their placement and individual parameters.

Correcting Notes with Notes

Note objects are ideal for the Auto-Tune effect. They are also ideal for simplifying your workflow in Graphical mode, since they do not allow the same level of tweaking Line and Curve objects offer. As covered in chapter 5, they are created either automatically via the Make Notes button or manually using the Draw Notes tool. (They can also be created via MIDI as shown in chapter 9.)

Making Notes with a Single Click

Like the Make Curve button, the Make Notes button is a fast and easy way to create Correction objects across your entire audio track, or just a portion of it when you've created a region with the I-Beam tool.

Make sure you have removed all previous Corrections objects before beginning this walk-through. For now, have the Green Output Curves hidden and the Red Curves visible. Your entire audio track should also be visible in the Pitch Graph display. Snap to Note is irrelevant, since Note objects are always created right on displayed pitch graph lines or lanes. They also take the current Scale setting into account when being created via the Make Notes button.

The goal of this walk-through is to experience the speed and ease Note objects bring to Graphical mode pitch correction.

1. Set Key and Scale as described in the previous walk-throughs (or set the scale to Chromatic), and this time you want Show Lanes clicked on.

2. Click the Make Notes button, located beneath the Pitch Graph display. You should now see a series of Note objects near most if not all Red Input Pitch Curves. Remember, Note objects are ideal for the Auto-Tune effect, and are not really designed for surgical pitch correction. Don't be surprised if your track contains several long Note objects that cover many notes or words in your source audio. That is not a bad thing.

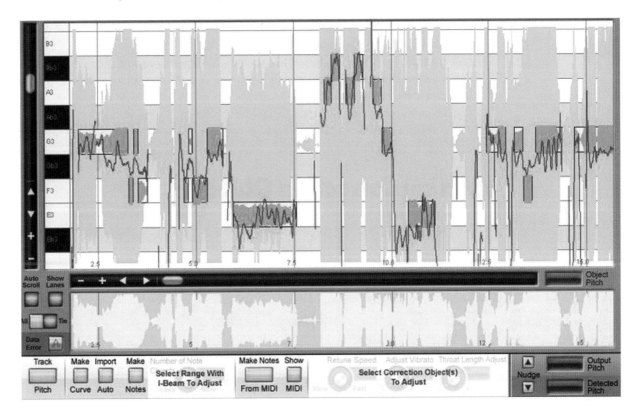

Figure 6.22

3. Without adjusting any other parameter, play back the audio to hear the results. Assuming the Default Retune Speed for these objects is set very fast, vocal effect pitch correction has been applied to your entire track in just a couple steps. Not bad, but let's make it better.

Number of Note Objects

With the entire audio track visible in the Pitch Graph display, turn the Number of Note Objects knob, located just to the right of the Make Notes button, fully clockwise and counterclockwise to see how it affects Note object creation in relation to the Red Input Pitch Curves.

Figure 6.23

Set to its maximum, even slight variances in pitch can receive Note objects. Set to its minimum, and you'll end up with fewer and longer Note objects across the track.

The default setting for Number of Note Objects is usually a great place to start (you have little choice here, since this parameter is not available until either you have used the Make Notes button or selected a region with the I-Beam tool). Too many Note objects, and vibrato and other vocal nuances will suffer by having multiple Note objects assigned to them. Too few usually means some transition notes that could possibly benefit from pitch correction will be ignored, and some Note objects will be long, thus impeding any transparent pitch correction efforts (though if your goal is transparent pitch correction, Curve objects and Line objects are a better choice).

When the Number of Note Objects parameter is set toward Less, Note objects are created based on the following:

- Small variations in pitch will not receive multiple Note objects relative to those variations.
- Large cyclical variations in pitch are treated as vibrato and therefore will receive a single Note object.
- Gradual pitch changes are seen as transitions and will not receive any Note objects.

When the Number of Note Objects parameter is set toward More, Note objects are created based on the following:

- Small variations of pitch will receive Note objects for those variations.
- Transitions are treated as glissandos, and will receive a Note object for every pitch detected in the transition.
- Vibrato passages will receive notes for different pitches within the vibrato.

Note objects are discussed in depth in chapter 10, which covers their use for mastering the Auto-Tune vocal effect.

Mixing Correction Objects

Graphical mode lets you use all three Correction objects on a single audio track. Take advantage of this flexibility when you are working in Graphical mode. Mixing up your Correction objects offers a high degree of flexibility.

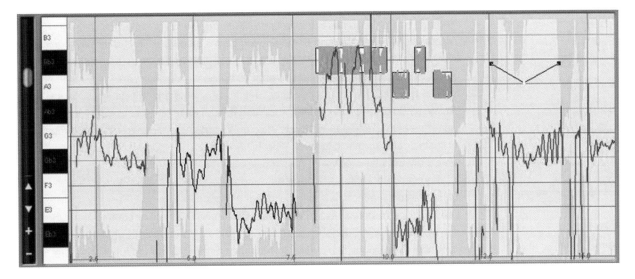

Figure 6.24

Correction Object Roundup

The following rule of thumb will help you determine which Correction object is ideal for any part of your track. And as always, rules are meant to be broken, especially in rock 'n' roll.

- Curve objects offer surgical precision and pitch correction transparency, and a speedy workflow, since they can be created automatically.
- Line objects are highly flexible, thanks to their segmentation capabilities. And while they cannot be created automatically, they too accommodate a speedy workflow since they can be segmented. Lines with multiple segments work great over long notes and passages with multiple pitches.
- Note objects are ideal for the Auto-Tune effect, and simplified correction processing in Graphical mode.

Thanks to that Retune Speed knob, all Correction objects can deliver when using Auto-Tune for effect purposes.

Using Auto Mode and Graphical Mode Together

As shown earlier in this chapter, a common workflow methodology and an excellent way to combine the power of Auto-Tune's two modes is to start in Auto mode, dial in pitch correction to taste, and then track your audio in Graphical mode and import your Auto mode settings.

To grasp the full force of what this workflow offers, here's another workflow that incorporates both modes.

This workflow is designed to explore the effectiveness of using Auto mode and Graphical mode together.

1. Open Auto-Tune as an insert on the track you wish to apply pitch correction to, and from the Auto mode window, dial in pitch correction to your liking as described in chapter 4. Set the Retune Speed knob somewhere between 20 and 30 (feel free to repeat this quick walk-through at different Retune Speed settings). Once again, if you know your song's key, set it in Auto mode, and this time, set the Scale to either Major

or Minor. If you do not know your song's key, set Key to C and Scale to Major. Turn on Formant so that pitch correction in this walk-through will still sound natural, even if the output pitches are a full step or more away from the source pitch. While we're at it, let's incorporate some Create Vibrato settings. Like Scale and Key, these parameters can be imported from Auto mode into Graphical mode.

2. In Auto mode's Create Vibrato section, set the Shape setting to sine wave, Onset Delay to 500, Onset Rate to 350, and Pitch to 30. Leave all other Create Vibrato parameters to their default settings. Also make sure Auto mode's Natural Vibrato knob is set to 0, and Targeting Ignores Vibrato is set to off. (The Create Vibrato parameters do not always play nicely with Auto mode's Natural Vibrato controls.)

   Play back the audio with these Auto mode settings, and listen to how these Create Vibrato settings affect the audio being sent through Auto mode. Feel free to tweak the Create Vibrato settings (especially Onset Delay and Pitch) as needed to better suit your audio. Keep in mind that these settings should be obvious enough to easily see and hear how they are applied to Graphical mode via the Import Auto function.

3. Go to Graphical mode, and use its Track Pitch feature to track in the same audio file you were pitch correcting via Auto mode. If you already have audio here, use the Clear All button to remove it prior to tracking.

4. Once all the audio data used in Auto mode has been tracked into Graphical mode, adjust the vertical scroll bar and zoom controls so you can see all, or at least most, of the Red Input Pitch Curves. If need be, adjust the horizontal plus and minus buttons so you can see the entire waveform inside the Pitch Graph display. As you should know by now, if Auto Scroll is turned on, this will have happened automatically, and you need do nothing. If Auto-Tune is set to display Green Output Pitch Curves, turn this off.

5. Click on the Import Auto button located beneath the left-hand side of the Pitch Graph display. Those now familiar Blue Correction Object Curves will have appeared near the Red Input Pitch Curves showing detected input pitches. The exact location of these Blue Curves will, of course, vary based on the above Auto mode settings. They could be right on top of the Red Curves, or very close to them. This time, some Blue Curves will bear a strong resemblance to their related Red Curves, and some will not. In many cases, it is the longer curves that will look the most different. This is due to the Create Vibrato settings applied in Auto mode, which will have an impact on the contour of long Blue Curves, especially near the ends of these curves.

   Go ahead and bring in the Green Curves for a visual reference of the output pitch.

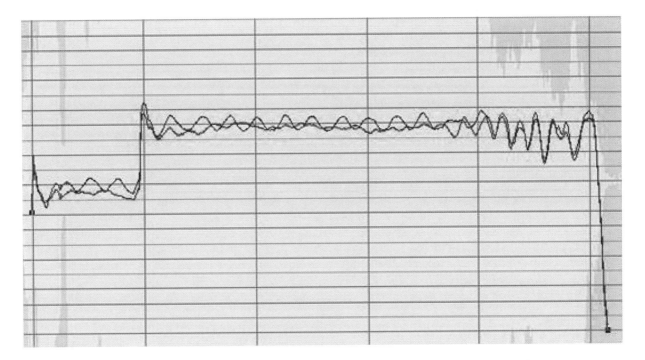

Figure 6.25

Of course, as you've experienced previously, each of these Correction objects can now be manipulated at your discretion, as described earlier in this chapter.

Think of this Auto-mode-to-Graphical mode workflow as Auto mode on steroids—you have applied pitch correction to the entire audio track in the Pitch Graph display as defined by how you have set Auto mode's parameters, while making each instance of pitch correction on that track available for independent and surgical pitch editing.

If you played back the audio after clicking on Import Auto, and prior to adjusting any of the Correction objects that click has created, then what you would hear in Graphical mode would be identical to what you were hearing in Auto mode assuming Auto mode and Default Retune Speeds matched.

Importing your Auto mode settings is a speedy way to apply surgical pitch editing, while preserving the effectiveness and simplicity of pitch correction via Auto mode. What's more, you can change any of the importable Auto Mode settings (shown below) and apply them to the audio inside the Pitch Graph Display simply by clicking the Import Auto button again. You do not need to clear data or retrack audio in order to do this. Remember, Import Auto can be applied to a specific region of audio selected by the I-Beam tool, or the entire track when no region has been defined. This makes the Import Auto function very powerful indeed.

Importable Auto Mode Parameters

When clicking on Import Auto in Graphical mode, the following Auto mode parameters are imported as part of Blue Curve Correction objects deposited in the Pitch Graph display.

- Key and Scale
- Retune Speed
- Scale Detune
- Edit Scale settings

The following Auto mode parameters are also imported via Import Auto if they have been adjusted or turned on:

- Targeting Ignores Vibrato
- Humanize
- Natural Vibrato settings
- Create Vibrato settings

Chapter 7

AUTO-TUNE LIVE

Released in summer of 2012, Auto-Tune Live is specifically designed for live use and therefore has lower latency than its Auto-Tune 7 counterpart. Since live performance is the focus, Auto-Tune Live does not have a Graphical mode. Auto-Tune Live still exists as a plug-in, and is not a stand-alone product. It is available in the same native audio plug-in formats as its predecessors (RTAS, VST, AU). It is not available in TDM. It is also Antares's first 64-bit plug-in.

Figure 7.1

Auto-Tune Live = Auto Mode

The interface for Auto-Tune Live is virtually identical to Auto-Tune 7's Auto mode, discussed in depth in this book. So much so that if you master the Auto mode chapter in this book (chapter 4), you will have largely mastered Auto-Tune Live.

The key addition that makes it a powerful tool for live use is its real-time MIDI functionality, outlined below.

Real-Time MIDI Control

Auto-Tune Live has a high level of MIDI continuous controller support over virtually all of its parameters. MIDI is ubiquitous in live music, even for bands that do not employ keyboards. And MIDI controllers, including foot pedals, have become much easier to program in recent years. Therefore, adding comprehensive MIDI support via continuous controllers gives artists at any level the ability to use Auto-Tune Live at their gigs, as long as they are comfortable with running a DAW during their set.

Auto-Tune Live's Real-Time MIDI Controls

MIDI information primarily uses note on and off data along with continuous controller (or "CC") data to do its thing. Namely, that thing is to play and manipulate in real-time sounds and parameters found in hardware and software sound modules and signal processors. The "CC" part of MIDI is integral to that manipulation, and Auto-Tune Live makes smart use of it.

In the Options dialog in Auto-Tune Live, you will find 16 different Auto-Tune Live parameters available for MIDI continuous controller assignment. Auto-Tune Live supports MIDI continuous controllers between 1 and 119. If you do not want to send continuous controller information to a parameter, then set the channel for that parameter to 0 or N/A (non applicable). N/A is also the default state of parameters in Auto-Tune Live's Options dialog.

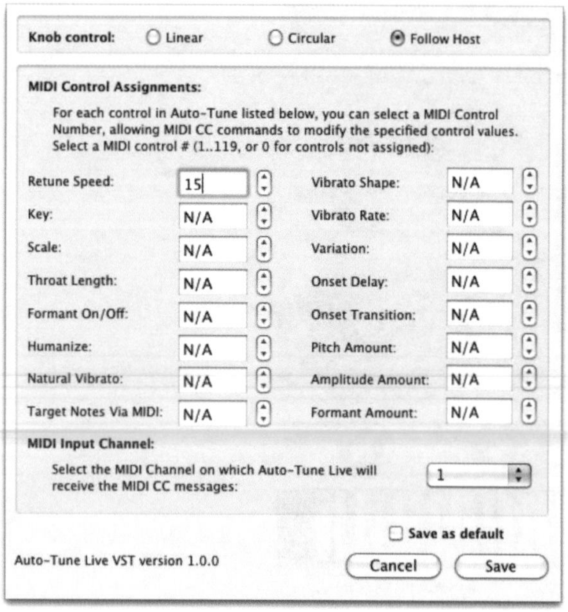

Figure 7.2

Once you have set the CC for any parameter in the Options dialog, sending MIDI data on the corresponding continuous controller from a MIDI controller or sequencer will cause the assigned Auto-Tune Live parameter to change in real time (as the continuous controller data is sent and received). Since Auto-Tune Live is a plug-in, that MIDI information can come from the DAW where Auto-Tune Live is placed as an audio insert, or external software or hardware MIDI devices connected to that DAW. Lots of options exist here, from foot pedals to smart-phone apps.

While Auto-Tune Live will let you set the same continuous controller on more than one parameter, setting the same CC on two Auto-Tune parameters can result in Auto-Tune Live behaving inconsistently. In other words, don't do that.

OMNI and MIDI Channels

Setting a continuous controller for any parameter only gets you halfway there. You also need to set the MIDI channel that you wish to send the data on. As you probably know, MIDI offers 16 different channels, or an Omni mode in which MIDI information will be accepted from any channel without a specific channel having to be set. Auto-Tune supports both individual MIDI channels and Omni mode.

At the bottom of Auto-Tune Live's Options window is a section where you can set the MIDI channel for incoming MIDI data. This is an important parameter, since you want to make sure Auto-Tune Live responds only to the MIDI data you intend to send it, and not MIDI data intended for another device sharing the same MIDI source as Auto-Tune. Whenever possible, select and dedicate a MIDI channel specifically for Auto-Tune Live.

MIDI Input Channel:

Select the MIDI Channel on which Auto–Tune Live will receive the MIDI CC messages: `1  ⬍`

Figure 7.3

Using Auto-Tune Live Onstage

Here's an example of using Auto-Tune Live's MIDI CC features in a live environment. Perhaps the chorus of your song employs the Auto-Tune effect, while the rest of the song calls for transparent pitch correction. The scale and key are the same throughout, so you only need to adjust the Retune Speed amount to get the Auto-Tune effect, and then adjust it back to return to transparent pitch correction.

Setting up a MIDI Controller and Auto-Tune Live

The above-described goal of adjusting Retune Speed during a live performance in order to engage the Auto-Tune effect on specific portions of a song is the kind of thing Auto-Tune Live is designed to accommodate with ease, as shown in the following walk-through.

1. Start by assigning a MIDI channel in Auto-Tune Live's Options dialog, so that the plug-in knows where to expect incoming MIDI data.

2. Next assign a CC to the Retune Speed field in the same Options dialog. Make sure you choose a CC that is not being used by other devices on the same MIDI channel using the same MIDI path as Auto-Tune. And to keep your MIDI programming clean, avoid commonly used continuous controllers reserved for things like MIDI volume (CC 7), MIDI pan (CC 10), and so forth. Refer to your MIDI device's MIDI implementation chart for help here.

3. Set the same MIDI CC assigned to the Retune Speed field inside Auto-Tune Live's Options window to a real-time controller on your external MIDI gear, or on a MIDI track inside your DAW. Likewise for the MIDI channel set in Auto-Tune Live.

4. Open your DAW's audio plug-in's MIDI routing section to assign the incoming MIDI data to Auto-Tune. While this will be different for every DAW, in many cases this routing setup can be found within the input and output section of the MIDI track dedicated for working with Auto-Tune Live.

Now when you adjust the assigned real-time MIDI controller on an external device (usually a knob, treadle pedal, or slider), or when your DAW plays the information from a MIDI track, Retune Speed values will change correspondingly.

A max value (127) from the real-time MIDI source will result in a 0 Retune Speed suitable for the Auto-Tune effect. Dialing back that controller from its maximum value will result in higher Retune Speed values suitable for transparent pitch correction.

Since the MIDI data ranges in value from 0 to 127, and Retune Speed ranges in value from 400 (the slowest Retune Speed setting) to 0 (the fastest Retune Speed setting), you will have to compare MIDI controller settings with Retune Speed values so you know exactly how far to adjust the real-time MIDI controller, or what data to program inside a MIDI track in your DAW.

MIDI Assignable Parameters in Auto-Tune Live

- Retune Speed
- Key
- Scale
- Throat Length
- Formant Correction On/Off
- Humanize
- Target Notes Via MIDI
- Vibrato Shape
- Vibrato Rate
- Variation
- Onset Delay
- Onset Transition
- Pitch Amount
- Amplitude Amount
- Formant Amount

In addition to real-time MIDI control, Auto-Tune Live also includes the same Target note MIDI capabilities found in Auto-Tune 7's Auto mode, as described in chapter 9.

Chapter 8
CREATING VIBRATO WITH AUTO-TUNE

Before you start working with vibrato in Auto-Tune, let me be clear about what vibrato is. Thanks in large part to Fender guitars and amps, vibrato is often confused with tremolo. Vibrato is a rapidly alternating change in pitch over time. Think of Stevie Nicks's vocals, and you will probably immediately think of vibrato. Think of the dramatically wavering notes singers employ when singing "The Star Spangled Banner" at a sports event, and you're thinking of vibrato. Tremolo, on the other hand, is a rapidly alternating change in volume. Link Ray's "Rumble" is a classic example of tremolo, as is The Smiths' "How Soon Is Now." Both of these guitar sounds were created using an external effect and not a vibrato bar on a guitar. That's right: even though many guitar companies and guitar players call the bar attached to the bridge of their guitars a tremolo bar (or in the vernacular of today's guitarist, a whammy bar), it is actually a vibrato bar, since it changes pitch and not volume.

Creating Vibrato After Tracking

As mentioned in chapter 4, the primary reasons for creating vibrato in Auto-Tune's Auto mode are twofold: either natural vibrato has been squashed by the pitch correction process, or the vocal is too static and needs a bit of variety to keep things sounding interesting. As we dive deep into vibrato creation via Auto-Tune, keep in mind that "interesting" is not always a good thing in popular music. Also keep in mind that without experimentation, the Auto-Tune effect might never have been employed in popular music.

As in most cases when manually adding something to a performance that should have already been there, or that was there but inadvertently removed, a little goes a long way. As an effect, vibrato creation can be put to good use adding character to recorded monophonic synthesizer parts. The information below applies to vocal parts as well as to instrumental parts.

Vibrato Research

Authentically creating vibrato manually requires a study of how singers use vibrato, and of course, no two singers use vibrato the same way. Before reaching for Auto-Tune's Create Vibrato controls, you need to know what vibrato style you are after. That takes listening to singers you admire, and songs that have a style you admire and that relate to the music you are working on. If you have any solo performances of a singer whose vibrato you wish to emulate, run that track into Graphical mode for analysis. Then you can see how fast and how wide those vibratos run, and you can use that information as a starting point for creating vibrato in Auto-Tune. It's important to temper expectations here. Unless you are going for a special effect, vibrato creation must be used subtly if it is to sound at all natural. That's not a bad thing, and less really is more sometimes.

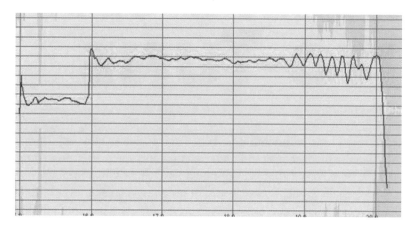

Figure 8.1. A Red Curve showing an unmistakable vibrato performance.

Vibrato and the Auto-Tune Effect

When setting the Retune Speed control to 0, thus creating the Auto-Tune vocal effect, vibrato present in the source audio will be removed—unless, as part of the effect, you've set Auto-Tune to assign Target notes or Correction objects to the distinct pitches found within that vibrato passage.

However, vibrato contains more than just changes in pitch. It also contains changes in formant and amplitude. So when applying a Retune Speed of 0 on a note that contains a strong vibrato, these other components of vibrato can sometimes be heard. Whether this works well with the Auto-Tune effect or not depends on the source material and is largely subjective.

Keep in mind that part of the sound of the Auto-Tune/Cher/T-Pain vocal effect is a lack of vibrato, or a mechanical-sounding one created by the pitch correction process. Long notes are often held static or assigned a melody by placing a series of Line or Note objects at different pitches over these long notes.

So if you know during the recording phase of your project that the Auto-Tune effect will be used on the vocal part along with melody creation, the singer should avoid using vibrato.

When pitch correction transparency is the goal, any unwanted removal of natural vibrato from the pitch correction process should be addressed by Auto-Tune's Natural

Vibrato knob before attempting to recreate vibrato under the Create Vibrato section (you can use Graphical mode's Import Auto feature to apply Natural Vibrato settings to audio inside the Pitch Graph display). It can also be addressed using Graphical mode's precision editing features, or simply by decreasing Retune Speed.

Creating Natural-Sounding Vibrato in Auto Mode

Figure 8.2

The Create Vibrato controls in Auto mode work in concert with one another. This makes dialing in vibrato a nonlinear workflow. Dialing up some parameters is often followed by dialing down others as you seek vibrato parameter equilibrium. Upon creating a nice vibrato effect, be sure to save the settings and create an Auto-Tune preset by saving the project and using your DAW's plug-in preset dialog.

Vibrato Shape

The sine wave is ideal for a natural-sounding vibrato. For special effects, try the square wave. The vibrato Shape parameter is also what turns on the Create Vibrato section.

Pitch, Amplitude, and Formant Amounts

It is recommended that you leave these parameters at their default settings and then revisit them as needed once you have dialed in the other Create Vibrato parameters. As mentioned above, while vibrato is defined as a pitch effect, amplitude and formant also play significant but subservient roles. Unless you are going for tremolo instead of vibrato, the amplitude changes in your vibrato should always be less than the pitch changes. Amplitude's default setting serves this nicely in many instances.

Vibrato Rate

This is the speed of the vibrato effect. Keep in mind that the rate or speed of a good vibrato has a relationship with the tempo of your song. Also keep in mind that real vibratos change in rate over time, often speeding up (and sometimes slowing down) near the end of the note receiving the vibrato effect. Onset Delay and Onset Rate go a long way in handling this important characteristic of natural-sounding vibrato. Another option is to use your DAW's automation controls to automate the Create Vibrato's Rate knob, turning it up slightly as the note plays out. This is a quick and easy approach to achieving this key characteristic of vibrato.

Variation

This parameter adds variation to the Create Vibrato's Rate and Amount settings. Just as the natural vibrato of a singer sounds error free, so should the Variation setting when employed. In other words, if you can hear the inconsistencies this parameter applies, it's probably set too high. If the created vibrato sounds mechanical, then it is probably set too low. Much like audio compression, a proper Variation setting means the changes this parameter adds to the vibrato you are creating are not obvious, and instead you just hear a pleasing-sounding vibrato.

Onset Delay and Onset Rate

The best singers ease in their vibrato. Onset Delay and Onset Rate emulates this practice when you create vibrato using Auto-Tune. Onset Delay establishes how long a note is sung before the Create Vibrato settings kick in. Onset Rate defines how long it takes, once the vibrato effect has begun, to reach the values set for Pitch, Amplitude and Formant Amounts. Experimentation is key to getting the most out of these settings, since they all work together. It also requires an understanding of the duration of the notes you wish to affect.

For example, if the note you wish to create vibrato for is 3 seconds long, and you have set both Onset Delay and Onset Rate to their maximum values of 1.5 seconds, then these settings will not allow the full range of Create Vibrato's Pitch, Amplitude, and Formant Amounts to be reached on that 3-second note. This is not necessarily a bad thing, and here's what happens: During that 3-second note, the Create Vibrato section starts applying its settings halfway into the note at the 1.5-second mark (as dictated by Onset Delay's 1.5-second setting). Since Onset Rate is also set to 1.5 seconds, Create Vibrato's Pitch, Amplitude, and Formant Amount settings start increasing toward their full values over the remainder of the note, which is also 1.5 seconds long. Therefore, the full values established for these Create Vibrato controls will be reached at the same moment the note ends.

Natural vibratos in a vocal part are rarely ever identical, but they should sound related, since they are sung by the same performer. Vibratos are sung differently based on many factors, including the length of the note. Therefore, the above Create Vibrato settings allow for different but related vibratos based on the length of each note held long enough for at least some vibrato effect to be applied, with only the longest notes receiving the full Create Vibrato settings—something to keep in mind when setting your Create Vibrato parameters in Auto mode.

Vibrato Automation

Today's DAWs make applying automation to plug-ins a breeze. Using the Create Vibrato section of Auto-Tune for creating natural vibrato effects is aided by the sensible use of plug-in parameter automation. All eight parameters in the Create Vibrato Control section can be automated. Here are some pointers on using automation for creating a natural-sounding vibrato.

- **Shape:** Changing the shape of the vibrato as it nears its peak can have dramatic results.
- **Pitch and Rate:** Slight changes of one or both of these parameters can be used in lieu of or in conjunction with Create Vibrato's Onset Delay and Rate parameters to emulate a natural-sounding vibrato technique.
- **Amplitude and Variation:** Decreasing or increasing these parameters toward the end of a created vibrato can be very effective on slow or quiet passages.
- **Onset Delay and Onset Rate:** Using automation to ride these parameters can keep multiple created vibratos from sounding too similar.

Vibrato Management

When it comes to vibrato management, whenever possible, choose either Natural Vibrato (working on the vibrato found in the source audio) or Create Vibrato, and not both. These sections are not designed to work together. Both work independently of Auto mode's pitch correction parameters, so using them together can cause all kinds of crazy things to happen audio-wise; though who knows, maybe there is some musical effect waiting to be discovered here.

It also bears repeating that creating vibrato manually with Auto-Tune is in most cases a last resort. Setting your pitch controls properly or automating them, especially the almighty Retune Speed control, can help preserve a natural vibrato. And that is something worth striving for—the same goes for the surgically precise pitch editing available in Graphical mode.

When to Use Targeting Ignores Vibrato

If vibrato performances that are part of the track being pitch corrected sound warbly and unmusical due to Auto-Tune attempting to pitch correct the notes found within that vibrato, turning on this parameter can sometimes help. Success with this parameter is based on the vibrato performance itself, making it a hit-or-miss kind of setting. Since this parameter is either on or off, it is easy to use and to A/B the results to see if it does help in such instances. If it does not, you can try taming the vibrato part by setting the Natural Vibrato knob toward its minimum settings. If that does not solve it, then Graphical mode work is probably required. That can be as simple as moving or removing Correction objects placed on the troublesome vibrato, or adjusting Retune Speeds for the part in question. Targeting Ignores Vibrato is one of the Auto mode settings imported into Graphical mode via the Import Auto function.

Figure 8.3

Vibrato Control in Graphical Mode

Vibrato management in Graphical mode is on a per-object basis. You can create vibratos manually by editing Correction objects, and you can control existing vibrato with the per-object Adjust Vibrato knob.

Adjust Vibrato in Action

Vibrato Adjust lets you adjust the width of a vibrato's pitch detected in the source audio. What the Natural Vibrato knob is in Auto mode, the Adjust Vibrato knob is on a per-object basis in Graphical mode. With subtle vibratos, changing Adjust Vibrato values may not be obvious to your ears. So let's use the Green Output Curves to help us understand what is happening here.

1. Track audio into the Pitch Graph display, and use the Make Curve button to create Curve Correction objects. Curves are ideal objects when working with this per-object control. We don't need to be too picky here, as the focus is on seeing how Adjust Vibrato affects output pitch.

2. Select one or more Correction objects (ideally choose ones placed on top a note containing vibrato), show the Green Output Pitch Curves, and then turn the Adjust Vibrato knob in either direction and watch those Green Curves.

3. Notice that at higher settings, the peaks and valleys of the output curve's contours will widen, probably drastically so. This shows you that vibrato width has been increased, thanks to the higher Adjust Vibrato settings. Play back the audio to hear the results of this setting. At this extreme setting, it may not sound very musical, so try scaling it back to taste.

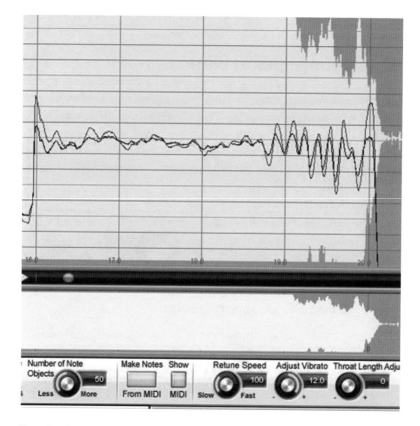

Figure 8.4. Green Output Pitch Curves show a widening of vibrato due to turning up the Vibrato Adjust parameter.

4. Now reduce Adjust Vibrato amount to its minimum value. Depending on the source audio and its vibrato, you will most likely see a narrowing of the Green Curve contour, and in some cases, the entire Green Curve may move down in pitch compared to the Red Input Pitch Curve as Auto-Tune attempts to constrain vibrato width. The lower the Retune Speed, the more dramatic these changes will be. Again, play back the audio to hear the results.

Dialing In Vibrato in Graphical Mode

When working with the Adjust Vibrato parameter, Try placing specific Correction objects individually on the vibrato portions you wish to pitch correct, give them a slow Retune Speed, and then dial in Adjust Vibrato to taste (with a slow enough Retune Speed, you may not need any vibrato adjustments).

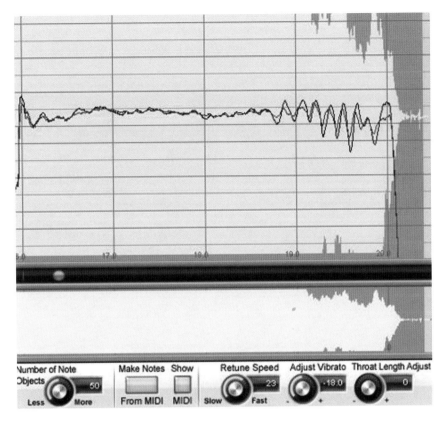

Figure 8.5. Green Output Pitch Curves show a reduction in vibrato width due to turning down the Vibrato Adjust parameter. Retune Speed has been increased to help reflect this change.

Keep in mind that removing pitch correction objects altogether from the vibrato section of the source audio, when practical to do so, is a sensible workflow methodology. Pitch correction is not a tool to be used heavy-handedly, unless your goal is an effect. Central to the power of Graphical mode is its ability to select precise notes or sections for pitch correction. Take advantage of this level of control wherever possible.

Creating Vibrato in Graphical Mode

You can also use the Curve tool to draw in a vibrato. While technically this is not a natural vibrato, since pitch is the only parameter being affected, you may find it works better than per-object parameter adjustments to vibrato present in the source audio. Make sure you have zoomed all the way in on the vertical axis to give you optimum control over the curve-drawing process. When drawing vibrato, keep peaks and valleys of the curves relatively small (less than a semitone in width). The more subtle the vibrato you draw, the better chance it will fit in with the performance.

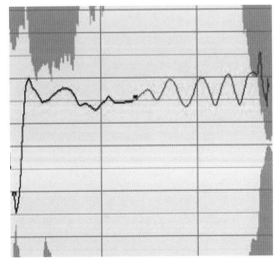

Figure 8.6. Since the vibrato portion of this note is on pitch, the Curve object was cut at the beginning of the vibrato section, and the part remaining over the vibrato was removed.

Chapter 9
MIDI AND AUTO-TUNE

Since Auto-Tune relies on settings for pitch and scale in order to properly pitch correct, using MIDI with the plug-in is a no-brainer. As you will see, feeding Auto-Tune MIDI notes is a fast and accurate way to establish Correction objects and Target notes.

For MIDI to work at all with Auto-Tune, your DAW must be able to route MIDI information to audio plug-ins. Most but not all DAWs support this. It's best to check your DAW's owner's manual to learn how to route MIDI to audio plug-ins before getting too far down the MIDI Auto-Tune path.

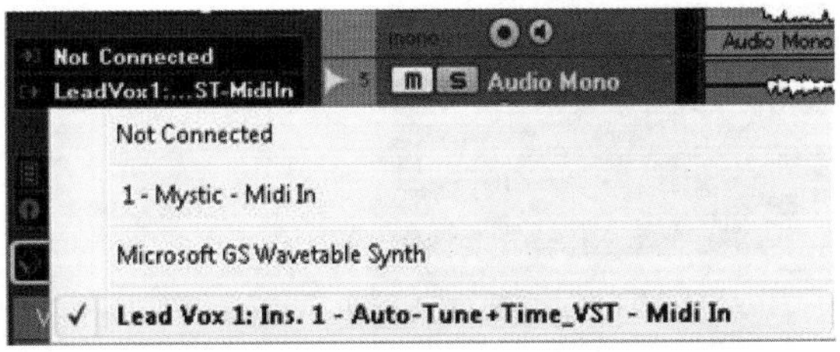

Figure 9.1. In Cubase, audio inserts are available in the MIDI output drop-down menu.

MIDI and Auto Mode

Auto mode has two MIDI modes—Learn Scale From MIDI, and Target Notes Via MIDI. The goal for both is to establish scales and Target notes from MIDI instead of the traditional Scale and Key parameters at the top of the Auto mode window. However, Target Notes Via MIDI only works while you are running audio through Auto mode; any Target notes established with this mode are released once the MIDI information stops being sent to the plug-in. Examples of using both of these features are covered below.

Keep in mind that when working with MIDI in Auto mode to create scales and Target notes, the right notes from your MIDI source are all that matter, and melody and timing do not. This is because as the source audio is played through Auto mode, it will correct based on proximity to these notes established by this MIDI information.

Learn Scale From MIDI

As covered earlier, determining the key of the music against which you wish to apply Auto-Tune and choosing the correct scale for the vocal part can be tricky for those without music-theory training. And while minor and major scales are the most popular scales used in Western modern music, many songs employ accidentals—notes outside the key's minor or major scale found in the song. The easiest way to deal with instances in which the key for the song and the scale for the melody are not readily apparent is via Auto-Tune's Learn Scale From MIDI feature. Learn Scale From MIDI is also a great way to lock down pitch correction to specific notes of a melody. It takes all the guess work out of melody creation when employing the Auto-Tune effect. And it simplifies setup when your aim is transparent pitch correction.

Whatever your needs are, the following walk-throughs will help you understand the power of MIDI in Auto mode.

Using Learn Scale From MIDI

With your MIDI keyboard or MIDI track routed to Auto-Tune, click the Learn Scale From MIDI button near the bottom left of Auto-Tune's Auto mode window. When engaged, it will light up blue, all the keys shown in the virtual keyboard will be grayed out, and the notes shown in the Key Edit display will be set to Remove.

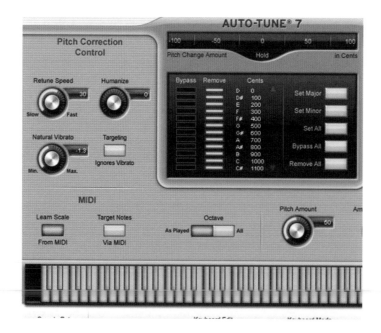

Figure 9.2

Play a vocal part through Auto mode, and play the notes found in the melody that you wish to pitch correct to on your MIDI keyboard (you can also record or create this information on a MIDI track in your DAW and play it in that way), and watch

Auto-Tune. If MIDI is routed correctly, you should see keys on Auto-Tune's Virtual Keyboard turn white or black, based on the notes Auto-Tune has received via MIDI. If under the Octave section the All button was selected, then these same notes should no longer be set to Remove in Auto-Tune's Edit Scale display.

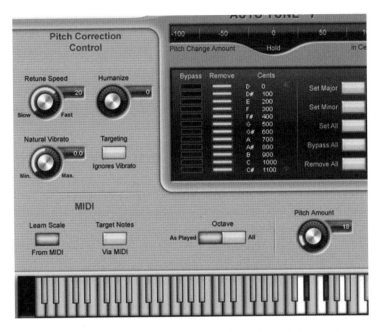

Figure 9.3. Target notes created via MIDI are shown in the Virtual Keyboard but not in the Edit Scale display, since the Octave As Played button was selected.

Figure 9.4. Target notes created via MIDI are shown on the Virtual Keyboard and in the Edit Scale display, since the Octave All button was selected.

Using MIDI, you have just defined for Auto-Tune the scale it will use for pitch correction. If you have Octave All engaged, and therefore created a custom set of Target notes inside the Edit Scale display, you can save this as an Auto-Tune scale by creating an Auto-Tune preset using your DAW's plug-in preset dialog, and then saving your project.

This is an excellent example of how Auto mode in Auto-Tune is powerful, yet yielding to a speedy and simple workflow.

Using Target Notes Via MIDI

Click on Target Notes Via MIDI, and press Play on your DAW. As it plays back audio and sends your vocal through Auto-Tune, play your MIDI keyboard (you can also use a MIDI track as described above). As you feed these notes to the plug-in while the track is rolling, Auto-Tune will use them to define the Target notes for pitch correction, but only as they are played. When these notes are stopped, no Target notes or scales will be remembered or established, and Auto-Tune defaults back to a state in which no Target notes are present.

When working with the Auto-Tune vocal effect, this is a great way to experiment with different melodies for the vocal part being affected. It also provides a high degree of flexibility with regard to establishing what notes are used in the pitch correction process. Since it does not remember any notes fed to it, this feature is ideal for creating simple or complex melodies in real time. In this instance, you will get the most out of your melody experiments if you play the melody from your MIDI source in time with playback of audio through Auto mode.

Target Notes Via MIDI lets you (or your sequencer) play the exact notes you want to correct to at the exact time you want them corrected, but this is not a requirement. Holding down keys on your MIDI controller, or creating MIDI notes that run the length of the vocal part on a MIDI track during playback, will also create these temporary Target notes. The Octave All button has the same effect on Target notes in the Edit Scale display as Learn Scale From MIDI, though these notes are not remembered by Auto-Tune when the MIDI data is not present.

MIDI support in Auto mode is key to melody creation when using Auto mode for effect purposes, and can really simplify the task of selecting the right notes, regardless of scale.

MIDI and Octave Mode

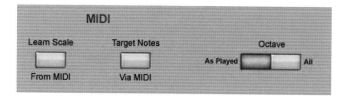

Figure 9.5

In most cases, and nearly all cases for melody work, MIDI modes in Auto mode should have Octave mode set to As Played. This keeps that incoming MIDI data octave specific. However, when using MIDI to create a custom Auto mode scale, you may want all octaves covered, not just the one containing the MIDI data. Just select All under the Octave mode to make this happen. Octave All must be set if you wish to save the Target notes created using Learn Scale From MIDI as a custom scale.

Turn off MIDI Features When Done

When using MIDI in Auto mode, its initial state will set Auto-Tune so that all Target notes are removed, causing the plug-in to not pitch correct anything. Because of this, accidentally engaging MIDI in Auto mode or forgetting to turn it off when done are great ways to drive yourself crazy.

Working with MIDI and Graphical Mode

MIDI in Graphical mode is designed to assist in the creation of Note objects, and like its use in Auto mode, this can really simplify the job of selecting the right key and scale for pitch correction and melody creation.

Keep It Monophonic

MIDI data coming into Graphical mode must always be monophonic. Because of this, take care to play your MIDI parts monophonically. Or better yet, record them on a MIDI track in your DAW before sending them to Auto-Tune, and then edit the MIDI data as needed to ensure it is monophonic.

Tracking Audio with MIDI

Graphical mode can only accept incoming MIDI data while it is tracking audio. If you select Show MIDI (located under the Pitch Graph display and to the left of the object-based Retune Speed knob), then upon completion of audio tracking, along with the Red Input Pitch Curves you're now familiar with, red boxes will appear in the Pitch Graph display showing you the location and pitches where MIDI notes have been captured.

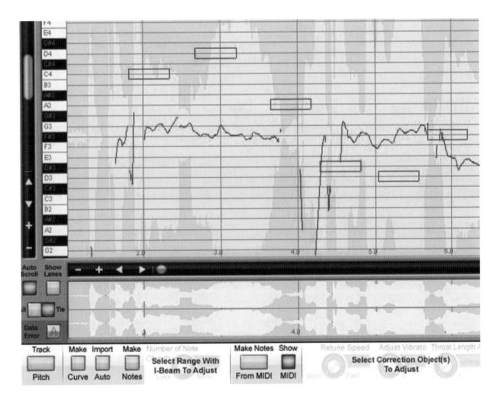

Figure 9.6

Make Notes From MIDI

Once you have successfully captured MIDI notes into Graphical mode, you can use this data to create Note objects. Simply click on the Make Notes From MIDI button, located beneath the Pitch Graph display. This is a fast and effective way to use keyboard parts as a basis for recreating melody, or defining target pitches and scales in Auto-Tune.

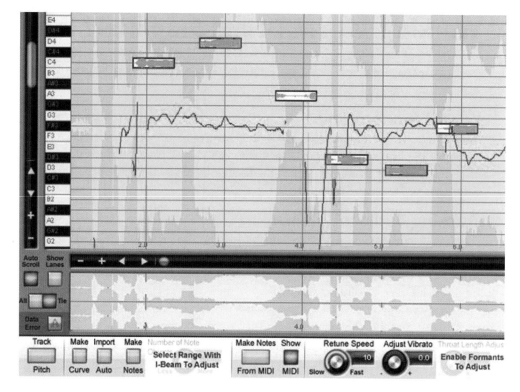

Figure 9.7

MIDI in the Pitch Graph Display

If your MIDI data contains a note that is not part of the current scale and key, the MIDI note data will get captured into the Pitch Graph display accurately (the MIDI note graphic representation will match that of the actual MIDI data), and therefore, pitch correction will get applied correctly. However, Object Pitch display will reflect that the MIDI notes are not part of the current Scale and Key. For example, if you track in a D♯ MIDI note and your Key and Scale is set to D major, then Object display will show D + 100 cents (which equals D♯, since 100 cents equals 1 semitone) and not D♯, since D♯ is not in the D major scale.

Chapter 10
MASTERING THE AUTO-TUNE VOCAL EFFECT

The Auto-Tune effect has been around since 1998, and if anything, its popularity has increased since that time. If you make popular music, or you plan on making a living as an audio engineer or producer of pop music, you need to know how to create this effect.

Using Auto Mode to Create the Auto-Tune Effect

While Graphical mode provides comprehensive control for achieving the Auto-Tune effect, you can quickly dial in the same popular effect in Auto mode with excellent results. In fact, Auto-Tune EFX 1 and Auto-Tune EFX 2 seem built with this purpose in mind, given its hard and soft EFX switch settings. This walk-through will focus on Auto-Tune 7, though the steps could apply equally to any version of Auto-Tune.

Keep in mind that a primary component of the Auto-Tune effect is melody editing and creation. Auto mode allows for limited melody work via Target note selections, while Graphical mode offers practically limitless melody work.

The Power of Retune Speed

Retune Speed allows you to set, in milliseconds, how quickly pitch correction is applied. At its fastest settings, subtle variations in pitch that make speaking and singing voices sound— well—human are removed, and instead, the

Figure 10.1

spoken or sung part is quantized exactly to the pitch defined by Auto-Tune's Target notes and pitch correction objects. This makes it the key parameter for achieving the Auto-Tune/Cher/T-Pain/Black Eyed Peas/Kanye West/"Auto-Tune the News" effect.

To get the Auto-Tune effect, simply turn the Retune Speed knob to 0 milliseconds, its fastest setting. This causes Auto-Tune to quantize the source material to exact pitches as described above, thus delivering the well-known effect. We can stop here in many cases, as you will find that simply setting Retune Speed to 0 delivers a good dose of the Auto-Tune effect. But since this book is about mastering Auto-Tune, here are a few more tips to give you the best possible Auto-Tune effect in Auto mode.

The Wrong Key Opens the Right Door

The greater the difference between the source pitch and the corrected pitch, the more pronounced the Auto-Tune effect will be. Keep that in mind not just when applying pitch correction but also when recording performances that will be receiving the Auto-Tune effect treatment. So if you really want a heavy Auto-Tune effect, try recording the vocal in a different key or octave than that of the final mix, and then set Key and Scale to that of the final mix when doing the Auto-Tune processing (and of course, set the Retune Speed control to 0).

When tracking vocals in a different key or octave than what will be used for the final mix, do your singer a favor and transpose backing tracks accordingly. Since the Auto-Tune effect is often backed by electronic music played via MIDI, changing the key to the song in advance of recording the vocal parts can be trivial. Simply use your gear's various transposition options, or move the MIDI data firing off those notes to different notes. Experimentation is the key here (pun intended). In fact, without experimentation, the Auto-Tune effect might never have been discovered.

Transpose Down, Then Tune Up

In situations where the vocal has already been recorded, using Auto-Tune's Transpose feature can sometimes strengthen the presence of the Auto-Tune effect. How well this works depends largely on the source material. Since it's easy to do, here's a walk-through explaining how.

1. Solo the vocal track destined for the Auto-Tune effect so it's the only one heard during this walk-through. Use Auto-Tune's Transpose knob to transpose the vocal track at least two semitones down (transposing between four and six semitones can also be effective). Remember, the Transpose knob's value are in semitones.

2. Set Retune Speed to its slowest setting and Bypass all Target notes inside the Edit Scale display. Our goal here is only to transpose, and then use a separate instance of Auto-Tune to create the vocal effect.

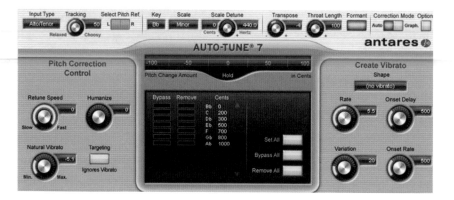

Figure 10.2

3. Mix down this audio track with Auto-Tune transposition applied, and then import it onto an empty track in your project; or if your DAW supports it, record the Auto-Tune output onto a new audio track in your project.

4. Place a new instance of Auto Tune on the newly created audio track that contains the transposed version of the Auto-Tune effect.

5. In this new instance of Auto-Tune, set Key and Scale to suit the melody and the song, set Retune Speed to 0, and adjust the Transpose knob to return the vocal back to the original pitch (i.e., if you set Transpose to -4 in step 2, set it to +4 now). Again, make sure Formant is turned on in this instance of Auto-Tune as well. Play back the results. What you should hear is a more intense version of the Auto-Tune effect at the right pitch and key for the song.

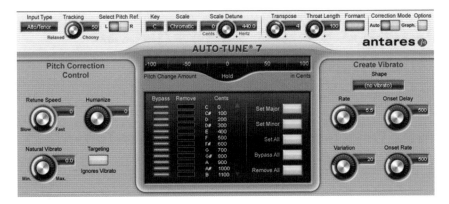

Figure 10.3

The above workflow is well suited for experimentation—try transposing the audio in opposite directions, or experiment with different Transpose settings or different Retune Speeds somewhere between 5 and 0.

The same results from the above walk-through could also have been accomplished by placing two instances of Auto-Tune on the tracks, each with the settings described above. Due to plug-in latency and the layers of processing, this setup, while easy, can be a bit glitchy, but since it's so easy to do, might as well give it a try.

Whether transposing down works better than transposing up depends largely on the source material. Higher-pitched vocals offer more room for transposing down, and lower-pitched vocals do not. In many cases, a single semitone can be enough to give your Auto-Tune effect the additional presence you seek. You can also track the transposed audio from step 3 into Graphical Mode and manually apply pitch correction using Note objects set to 0 Retune Speed. This method offers both an intense version of the vocal effect and supreme control over melody and pitch editing.

Transpose with Discretion

Transpose is a parameter that can easily send things careening to the abyss of bad processing, so try a few different settings to determine if this method works for your track or not. (And of course, experiment away—who knows, you may pioneer the next great vocal effect!)

As discussed previously, using Auto-Tune's Transpose feature usually requires engaging Auto-Tune's Formant control; otherwise your edgy gangsta rapper may sound like a silly cartoon mouse.

A Scalable Solution

Just like shifting keys can help deliver a more prominent Auto-Tune effect, so can changing scales. Keep in mind that many of the scales available from the Scale menu use pitches that fall outside of the A = 440 Hertz reference pitch common to Western music, so once again, experimentation is required.

Better still, start with the right scale for the melody of your vocal part, and then start removing notes, using either the Remove buttons in the Edit Scale display or, to keep these changes octave specific, the Virtual Keyboard (set Keyboard Edit to Remove) at the bottom of the Auto mode window. Both methodologies will force Auto-Tune to shift pitches above and below what would normally be the closest pitch in the scale. Sounds easy, and it is. Mastering this goes a long way in mastering the Auto-Tune effect in Auto mode.

Mastering the Auto-Tune Effect in Graphical Mode

With the use of Note objects, Graphical mode is a powerful environment for working with the Auto-Tune effect.

Using Note Objects for Melody and the Auto-Tune Effect

Here's a fast Graphical mode workflow methodology for creating the Auto-Tune effect that uses only the Note tool, the Scissors tool, the Arrow tool, and your imagination.

1. Track into Graphical mode a vocal part that is at least 30 seconds long. By now you should know how to set up Auto-Tune to accommodate this simple task. If not, back up and revisit chapters 5 and 6.

    Before tracking audio, select a scale and key that best fits the song. If none do, or you are not sure what the song's key is, select a chromatic scale. Also choose Show Lanes, which is very conducive to working with Note objects, and make sure the Formant switch is turned on. Using bars and beats as a time reference in your project will really help here, and you should use the same time reference in Auto-Tune. (This assumes your DAW is sending valid project time to the plug-in, and the timing of your song is based on your project's bars and beats time reference.)

2. Upon completion of tracking, use the horizontal plus and minus buttons to make sure all of the tracked audio is visible in the Pitch Graph display (if Auto Scroll is on, this will have happened automatically). If you cannot see the Red Input Pitch Curves, use the vertical scroll bar to make them visible.

3. Select the Note tool, and on a note lane at least a full step from the detected pitch (as shown by the Red Curves), draw a single Note object that covers the entire audio track shown in the Pitch Graph display. Remember, when you first create a Correction object, it uses the Retune Speeds set in the Options dialog. If your Note object Default Retune Speed setting is not 0, then use the per-object Retune Speed to set it to 0 now.

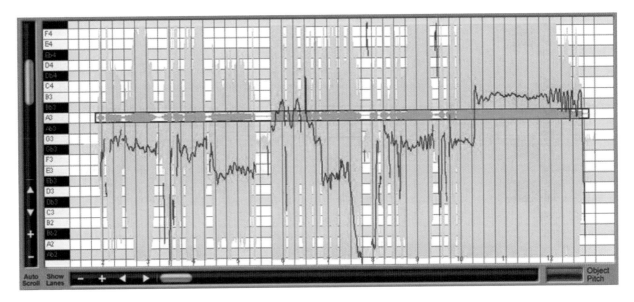

Figure 10.4

4. Select the Scissors tool, and cut up this single Note object into multiple sections of differing lengths (at least six for every 10 seconds of tracked audio). It doesn't really matter where you make your cuts at this point, since you will be changing them with ease later. However, cutting them on the bars and beats lines of the Pitch Graph display is a very musical choice, assuming they match the bars and beats of your project (they should).

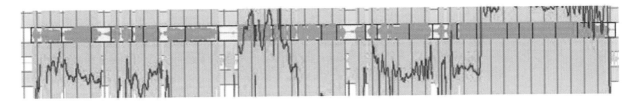

Figure 10.5

5. Now select the Arrow tool and begin moving Note objects to different pitches. You may want to zoom in to specific sections of audio, since the Arrow tool functionality changes based on where it is on a Note object. (Near the ends of Note objects, it shortens or lengthens the object; in the middle, it is set to grab them and move them vertically to different pitches.) Remember that to move objects horizontally, you need to hold down Control (Windows) or Option (Mac).

   If you have a melody in mind, move the Note objects to accommodate that melody. If you don't, just move to different notes at random; though for the sake of simplicity, keep those moves well within an octave.

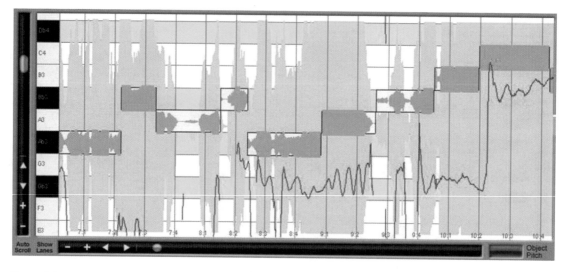

Figure 10.6

6. Make sure Auto-Tune's Formant control is turned on, and play back the audio to hear the results. You should now hear a classic example of the Auto-Tune/Cher/T-Pain effect—probably with unusual timing and melody unless you were lucky with your random cuts and movements or had moved pitches and made cuts with a melody in mind.

As you play back and listen, pay close attention to the Pitch Graph display. It should become obvious what Note objects require editing to tighten up those random cuts and pitches into a solid melody.

Since you can only have one Correction object at any given time in your tracked audio, extending the lengths from either the start or end of any Note object will automatically change the lengths of any adjacent Note objects as needed. As you will see when you play back your edits, this can really help speed up the editing process.

Again, this methodology lends itself to creative experimentation, so don't hold back.

If the effect is not dramatic enough, try moving the Note objects further away from the Red Curves.

Instead of drawing a single, long Note object in the above walk-through, you could have also used the Make Notes button and Number of Note Objects knob for creating Correction objects on the track. If you do not need to do any melody work, this would likely be a faster way to go, since Note objects will be created based on Scale and Key settings, thereby preserving melody while applying the Auto-Tune effect to the correct key and scale of the song.

MIDI and the Auto-Tune Effect

A powerful variation on the above example for creating the Auto-Tune vocal effect is to incorporate MIDI into the workflow.

As described in the previous chapter, Auto mode's Learn Scale From MIDI and Target Notes Via MIDI features are ideal for experimenting and capturing scales and melodies for your Auto-Tune effect work. Doing so in real time is a very creative process, since you can melodically jam along to the music. In our digital world of computer-based music production, it's sometimes easy to forget that the best part of making music is playing music. Creative juices, the muse, heartbreak—whatever it is that inspires you to create music, it's nearly always a real-time endeavor that exists in the moment. Auto mode's MIDI features respect that, as they are very performance-oriented features.

Keyboards and MIDI controllers are excellent tools for creating melodies, even for those not trained on the keys. Once you've defined your melody via your keyboard (and possibly your keyboard player), record it as a MIDI track into your DAW, and then route the output of that MIDI track to Auto-Tune. Before tracking into Graphical mode, you should examine the MIDI track and edit it as needed to make sure it is truly monophonic. Then track audio into Graphical mode while that MIDI melody is also being routed to Auto-Tune. Then click the Create Notes From MIDI button to create Note objects whose placement will be based on the captured MIDI data. Once those Note objects are created, adjust the Note object start and end points as previously described to fine-tune the melody to the vocal.

When tracking audio into Graphical mode, any MIDI data fed to Auto-Tune automatically gets captured, whether the Show MIDI button is on or off. This streamlines the MIDI to Note object workflow.

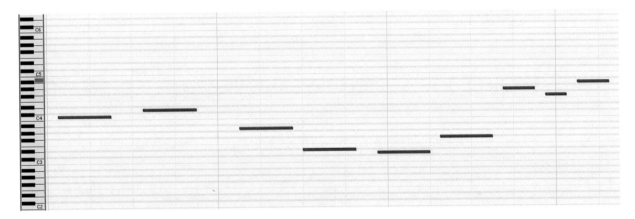

Figure 10.7. A monophonic MIDI part suitable for tracking into Graphical mode.

Chapter 11
AUTO-TUNE ON MUSICAL INSTRUMENTS

Technically, the human voice is a musical instrument, perhaps the most musical of them all. It is certainly the most complicated and unique. While two guitars or pianos may sound virtually identical, two vocalists never, ever will. Each voice is different, often dramatically so. Auto-Tune's success is in part due to how well it works despite these differences. But Auto-Tune can also be used on musical instruments such as bass, guitar, and wind instruments, provided the performance is monophonic and not polyphonic.

Monophonic Matters

When using Auto-Tune on a monophonic instrument part, there are a few things to keep in mind.

Wind instruments, like vocals, are truly monophonic. That is, they are largely incapable of playing more than one note at a time. Great. Auto-Tune is ready to go out of the box in such instances. But string instruments such as electric bass and electric guitar are polyphonic instruments that often play monophonic parts (this is especially true of bass and, of course, many guitar solos). When using Auto-Tune on a monophonic performance played on a polyphonic instrument, you are best served by using Graphical mode for surgically precise pitch correction.

In such instances, you need to listen closely to the audio you are working on to find instances where two or more notes overlap, and be sure not to have any Correction objects applied to these sections.

Setting up Auto-Tune for Musical Instruments

Auto-Tune's parameters are easily adjusted for musical instruments, and some are even designed for them.

Input Type

Be sure to set the correct Input Type for the instrument you will be processing with Auto-Tune. Bass Instrument is, of course, available as an Input Type, though if the bass part only contains pitches at the higher ends of the bass guitar frequency spectrum, you may also want to try the Instrument Input Type if source pitch detection is less than satisfactory.

Figure 11.1

Keep in mind that the Bass Input Type extends the frequency range for pitch detection down to 25 Hertz. Other Input Type settings only go as low as 55 Hertz (open A on a bass guitar). At a reference pitch of A = 440 Hertz, open E on an electric bass guitar is 41 Hertz. Keep these figures in mind when using Auto-Tune on bass and other instruments.

In most cases, the Instrument Input Type will be ideal for most musical instruments. However, Auto-Tune's pitch correction is only as good as its pitch detection, and selecting the correct Input Type along with the correct Tracking setting allows you to optimize the pitch detection part of the job.

Retune Speed for Instruments

Retune Speed, as you have already learned, is a key parameter for all forms of pitch correction. The first part of any note (the attack portion of the note envelope) plays a huge role in how we perceive that note, how we define it as a note from a bass guitar versus a piano, and so on. Too fast of a Retune Speed on musical instruments will nearly always result in unnatural-sounding pitch correction. (Remember, since Retune Speed is measured in milliseconds, the lower the number on the Retune Speed knob, the more quickly it applies pitch correction.) Retune Speed settings around the 25–35 range work best for most kinds of musical instruments. For instruments and performances with a very soft attack, slower Retune Speeds may be called for.

The per-object Retune Speed capabilities of Graphical mode make it an ideal mode for musical instruments, especially when the performance is complex. This is significant, since elongated notes with vibrato will require a different Retune Speed than eighth notes or 16th notes.

Keep It Real

Subtle amounts of "out-of-tune-ness" are essential to a natural-sounding performance. So while Auto-Tune makes it easy to achieve uniformly perfect pitch, it's not just okay to let through some small pitch errors; it may be a requirement, depending on the genre of music you are working with and the types of musical instruments selected by the artists or producer whose signature sound may be, in part, the result of less than perfect pitch. There are no hard and fast rules here, with the possible exception of folk, blues, and Americana music, which need to have obvious ties to their organic and simple roots. After all, this music was born at a time when tuners were not commonly available, and being in tune was quite subjective.

Also consider that some types of heavy metal are defined by high degrees of precision across all musical aspects, and other forms of heavy metal harken back to the slightly dissonant thunder of '70s hard rock. While both styles fit under the broad heavy metal umbrella, the pitch correction requirements for each will be dramatically different.

Graphical mode's Curve objects will provide the flexibility and precision for surgical pitch editing of non-vocal tracks in your project.

Drums tend not to work with Auto-Tune, since the waveforms are usually too short for Auto-Tune to detect source pitches with a high degree of accuracy.

Detune with Auto-Tune

If you or your clients use synthesizers and samplers for guitar and bass parts, or other parts that emulate analog instruments, Auto-Tune's Graphical mode can also be a powerful and handy tool for "roughing up" the pitches in those parts. Using synths and samplers for guitar parts is common, and when it sounds subpar, it's usually due to the part being too perfect, and therefore too sterile. Track that audio into Graphical mode, create Correction objects (Curve objects are a great place to start), and move some of those pitches a little off their pitch-perfect positions.

That's right, not only does Auto-Tune work great for putting performances on pitch, it can also be used to move things off pitch, making your guitar solos sound like they were played by a guitarist bouncing off the walls instead of a keyboardist sitting on the edge of the bed.

Experiments with Pitch

It has been noted repeatedly that art dies without constraints. It is likewise true that art cannot grow, indeed flourish, without experimentation. What happens if you track in a guitar part and use Auto-Tune's Throat Length and Transposition knobs to make that guitar part a bass part? Or if you use Auto-Tune's Key, Scale, and Transposition parameters on a copy of a (monophonic!) guitar solo track to double that solo and make it sound like it was played on two guitars—one beefy, one bright? What effect do Retune Speed and Throat Length have on a clarinet part that should really be a saxophone part? Imagine that staccato rock piano part doubled an octave down. Introduce a fretless bass into the project and just think of the possibilities! These are just a few examples of the kind of artistic experimentation Auto-Tune makes available for the various musical instruments in your project. And while mastering Auto-Tune involves knowing the rules of pitch correction and the limitations of the technology, it also involves knowing when to break those rules. Breaking new ground can be awfully fun.

Chapter 12
AUTO-TUNE TIME COMPRESSION AND EXPANSION

As of version 7, Auto-Tune included time correction along with its pitch correction capabilities. Time correction works in two distinct ways: moving forward or backward in time a specific point of audio such as a part of a syllable or a single note, and moving forward or backward an entire region of audio, such as a whole syllable, word, or phrase. In order to keep these time edits as natural sounding as possible, Auto-Tune constrains time editing to a ratio of 10:1. That means audio can be expanded up to 10 times its original length, or reduced by as much as 1/10th of its original length. And frankly, if you need more than that, well, you have bigger problems than Auto-Tune can solve.

Keep in mind that these constraints are applied cumulatively, and not per edit.

As discussed in chapter 2, when working with time editing, Auto-Tune always works on a copy of the original audio file. You can manage these copies via the Data File Management dialog, accessed via its button at the bottom of the Graphical mode window. Remember that when transferring a project that contains Auto-Tune time edits from one computer to another, you will need to use the Data File Management dialog to move any copies of audio files Auto-Tune has created (again, see chapter 2 for details on this).

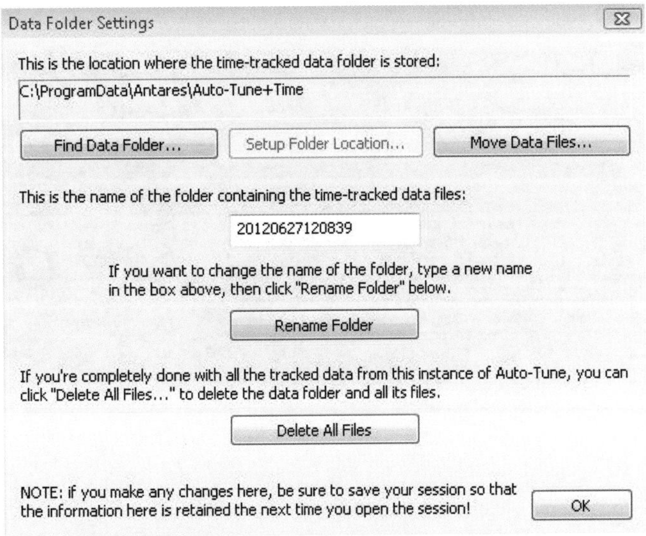

Data Folder Settings

This is the location where the time-tracked data folder is stored:

C:\ProgramData\Antares\Auto-Tune+Time

Find Data Folder...   Setup Folder Location...   Move Data Files...

This is the name of the folder containing the time-tracked data files:

20120627120839

If you want to change the name of the folder, type a new name in the box above, then click "Rename Folder" below.

Rename Folder

If you're completely done with all the tracked data from this instance of Auto-Tune, you can click "Delete All Files..." to delete the data folder and all its files.

Delete All Files

NOTE: if you make any changes here, be sure to save your session so that the information here is retained the next time you open the session!   OK

Figure 12.1

Also remember that when your project is done and delivered, you can delete these unneeded audio file copies via Data File Management.

Tracking Pitch and Time

For time editing, Auto-Tune offers a separate tracking button, labeled Track Pitch + Time, located beneath the Track Pitch button. If you plan on performing time edits, you must use Track Pitch + Time to track your audio into Graphical mode. As the button's name indicates, audio tracked this way can also receive pitch correction edits as necessary.

The process of tracking audio is identical between Track Pitch and Track Pitch + Time, the only difference being that the latter creates a copy of the audio file that Auto-Tune will work from.

Figure 12.2

Upon tracking audio for time edits, audio data in the Pitch Graph display will look the same as if you had tracked just for pitch correction. If Enable is set in the Time Control section, which it is by default, the Envelope Graph display will show two panes of the amplitude waveform separated by a red line. This red line means that any audio adjacent to it is available for time correction. When you start performing time edits, the top pane will also provide a visual reference showing you how the waveform has changed based on those edits, while the bottom envelope shows the original, unedited version of the waveform.

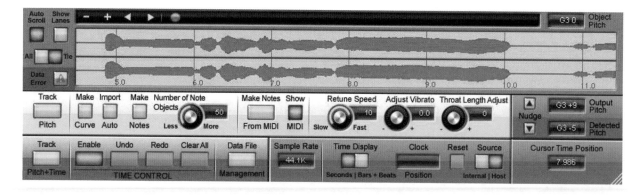

Figure 12.3

The Time Control Section

Since time manipulation is treated differently than pitch manipulation in Auto-Tune, it requires its own set of editing functions, located in the Time Control section.

Enable (Time)

The Enable button turns on time editing functionality and causes the aforementioned time editing view of the Envelope Graph display. The red line in the Envelope display remains visible whether Enable is on or off. However, when Enable is turned off, the Envelope Graph display will revert to displaying a single waveform, and the time tools will not function.

Toggling Enable on and off is a great way to A/B your time edits.

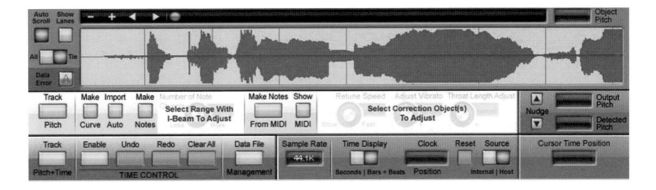

Figure 12.4

Undo (Time)

Similar to the Undo function for Pitch editing at the top left of the Graphical mode window, Undo under the Time Control section will undo the most recent time edit. For example, if you performed five time edits, you will need to click Undo five times to remove all five edits. As with the pitch editing Undo function, the number of undo's is managed in Auto-Tune's Options dialog. Undo becomes available once you have performed a time edit.

Redo (Time)

Clicking Redo returns any edit removed by clicking Undo. So continuing the above example, if you clicked Undo five times to remove five edits, you can click Redo five times to bring those edits back. If only real life were that simple. Redo is only available if you have used the Undo button.

Clear All (Time)

Clear All will undo with a single click all time edits you have performed. Clicking Undo after clicking Clear All will return edits removed by using the Clear All button. The Time Section Clear All only works on time edits, and does not clear pitch edits or audio tracked into the Pitch Graph display. If you wish to clear tracked audio, use Graphical mode's global Clear All, located in the top left of the Graphical mode window.

Auto-Tune's Time Tools

Time editing in Auto-Tune is done via two context-sensitive tools, the Move Point tool and the Move Region tool. Using these tools alone or in combination offers complete control of Auto-Tune's time manipulation.

Figure 12.5

The Move Point Tool

As its name implies, this tool allows you to move forward or backward in time a single point of audio. In order for this function to work, Auto-Tune must expand or compress the audio around the point being moved. Even within the 10:1 range available for time editing, the further you move a point of audio, the harder it will be for the edit to sound natural, though Auto-Tune generally does a good job in this area.

There are two steps involved with using the Move Point tool—selecting the region in which you will be working, and then moving the audio in time. The Move Point tool cursor will change icons to let you know which of the two moves it is ready to perform. If at any time your icon changes to a circle with a slash, then you have moved into an area not available for time editing purposes. Let's walk through using this tool.

The Move Point Tool in Action

This walk-through reveals how easy it is to use Auto-Tune's time editing feature using the Move Point tool.

1. Track in audio using the Track Pitch + Time feature. Ideally this audio should be a vocal that contains some rests or spaces between some of the words. You don't need to track in much, 10 seconds will be plenty for this walk-through.

   Upon stopping tracking into Auto-Tune, you should see in the Envelope Graph display two identical amplitude waveform displays with a red line between them. (Remember, the Time Control section Enable button must be turned on to see the two waveforms and to use the time tools.) Zoom in appropriately in the Pitch Graph display so that the audio you wish to perform a time edit on is viewable, along with several seconds of audio (or silence) on either side.

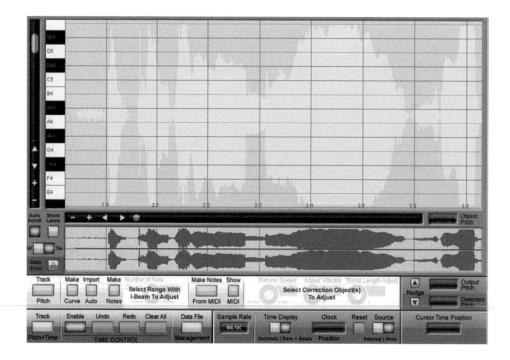

Figure 12.6

2. Select the Move Point tool, and place its cursor inside the Pitch Graph display. Upon the cursor entering the Pitch Graph display window, notice how it changes to an I-Beam. This is Auto-Tune telling you it is ready for you to select a region for time

editing. Similarly to how you use the I-Beam tool, select a region that contains the audio point you wish to move in time, the location you wish to move it to, and a few seconds on either side to provide a bit of breathing room. The selected audio will have a gray background. Notice that when you move your cursor within the region selected for editing, the cursor takes the shape of the Move Point tool icon, and outside the region, it changes back to an I-Beam. This tells you where you can move audio (the Move Point tool icon) and where you can select another region for editing (the I-Beam cursor).

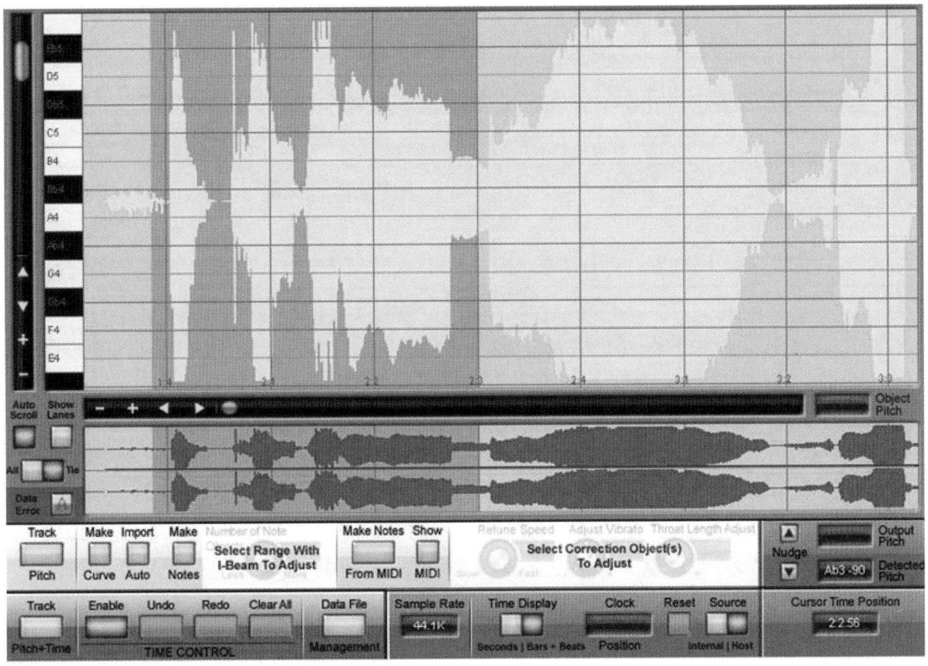

Figure 12.7

3. Select the point of audio you wish to move, and click and drag it to the location you wish to move it to. To gain a solid understanding of this tool's potential, select just one part of a syllable in a word, and move it forward or backward a quarter beat or less.

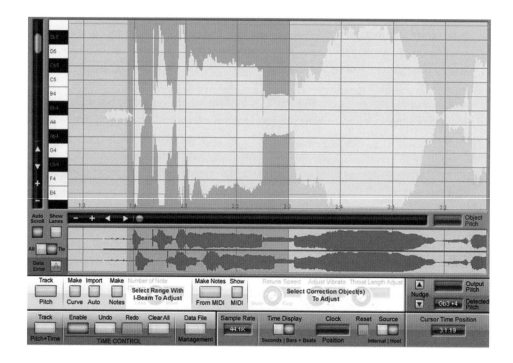

Figure 12.8. Look at the two waveforms in the Envelope Graph display to compare the time edit to the unedited source.

4. Play back the audio to hear the change. Remember, Auto-Tune will need to expand and compress the audio around the audio point moved, and the further you move it (depending largely on the type of audio surrounding it), the greater the chance that the edit may sound unnatural. Luckily, you have an Undo feature to help you experiment with your time edits.

Having rests or silence around the audio point you wish to use will help facilitate transparent time manipulation. As with any noisy audio tracks you plan on tracking into Auto-Tune, the track should be scrubbed prior to tracking for noises and unwanted sounds that are not part of the performance.

The Move Region Tool

The Move Region tool is used when you need to move a section of audio forward or backward in time, but you want to preserve the timing of the region selected for moving. Where the Move Point tool is designed to work with very small sections of audio down to a single point, the Move Region tool is designed to work on entire words, notes, or phrases you want to keep intact but move in time within the audio track. The emphasis here is on preserving the timing within the portion of audio being moved, while the audio around it is either compressed or expanded to facilitate the time edit.

There are three steps to performing a time edit with the Move Region tool—selecting the region of audio in which you will be working, selecting the region of audio to be moved, and of course, moving the audio region. Let's walk through using this tool.

The Move Region Tool in Action

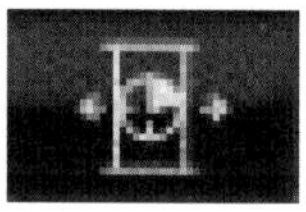

To help illustrate the difference between Move Region and Move Point tools, let's use the same section of audio you tracked for the Move Point tool walk-through. Hit Undo in the Time Control section until you have removed all your previous time edits (you can also just hit the Time Control section's Clear All button).

Figure 12.9

1. Select the Move Region tool. Notice that, like the Move Point tool, when you place it within the Pitch Graph display, its cursor turns into an I-Beam, letting you know you can define a region of audio within which you will be time editing. For this walk-through, select a large region of audio to help facilitate moving a region instead of a point.

   Once you have selected a region (again shown with a gray backdrop), the Move Region will turn into a double I-Beam cursor if you are within that selected region, and the standard I-Beam cursor outside of it. The double I-Beam cursor indicates that you can create a region of audio for moving within the overall region you created with the single I-Beam cursor.

2. With the double I-Beam cursor, select a region of audio to be moved. Since you moved a single point with the Move Point tool, select the entire word that contained that point for this Move Region tool walk-through.

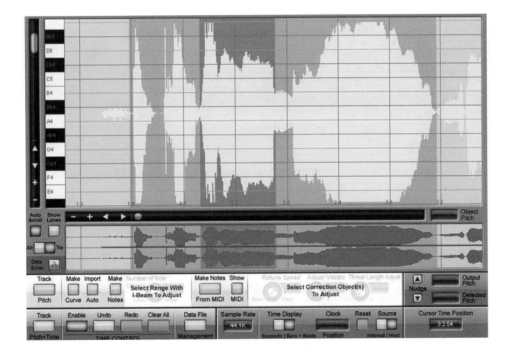

Figure 12.10

Now that you have selected a region (the word) of audio for moving in time, you have three potential cursors available (four if you count the circle-slash telling you you're beyond the boundaries of audio available for time editing): the single I-Beam and double I-Beam as described above, and the Move Region icon that will appear when the cursor is over the region of audio selected for moving.

3. Place the cursor over the region selected for moving (as shown by the Move Region cursor), and move it forward or backward within the defined time editing region.

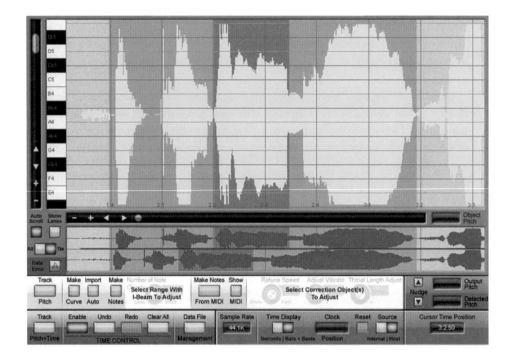

Figure 12.11

Once again, the two waveforms in the Envelope Graph display show the time edit compared to the unmodified source audio.

4. Play back the audio to hear the results. Use Undo to retry the edits and experiment with this tool.

Time Preserves Pitch

When editing time in Auto-Tune, any Correction objects that are present will be moved, compressed, and expanded in sync with any time edits. It is unlikely that a time edit will adversely affect any pitch correction edits previously applied. However, in the event that you need to change how you have applied pitch correction to audio edited for time, you can safely use the pitch correction editing tools above and immediately below the Pitch Graph display without affecting your time edits. This is an important point—time editing and pitch editing in Auto-Tune are completely independent of each other, with the beneficial exception that when audio that already has a pitch correction object applied to it is moved in time, those pitch correction objects will likewise get moved.

Picking the Right Time Tool

When very small sections of audio need to be time edited, it may be difficult to decide which of Auto-Tune's two time tools to use. The general rule of thumb is: The Move Point tool is ideal for moving a single point of audio, such as the attack portion of a note. However, the Move Region tool is designed for moving a region that contains timed elements, such as long notes whose attack, sustain, and release are distinct and should be preserved, or a word of one or more syllables.

The Data Error Indicator

Auto-Tune's time editing requires faster than real-time audio processing. While today's computers are lightning fast, complex projects containing high track-counts, lots of virtual instruments, and lots of audio plug-ins can stress even the most powerful computer. And working at high sample rates can seriously compound resource issues. If your DAW cannot keep up with the playback of your time edits, Auto-Tune's Data Error Indicator, located just above the Track Pitch button, will flash red. In most instances, you will also hear audio glitches when this occurs. If that happens, you may need to revisit the optimization information found in chapter 2, and if optimization does not help, then you need to make smaller time edits.

Figure 12.12

If the Data Error Indicator flashes but you do not hear any audio glitches, then the error may be so small as not to cause any streaming or processing issues, and you need do nothing, except perhaps render or mix down the track as soon as your time editing is complete. And as always, it's a good idea to copy the unaltered version of the track before edits are made permanent through mixing down or rendering.

APPENDIX: ABOUT THE DVD-ROM

Many of the walk-throughs found in *Mastering Auto-Tune* are also available as exercises on the included DVD-ROM. These DVD-ROM walk-throughs include additional tips and tricks that, along with the text and figures, will help you quickly master all forms of Auto-Tune pitch correction for your personal or professional studio. This DVD-ROM also includes detailed tours and explanations of the user interface for Auto-Tune Live, Auto-Tune EFX 2, and the flagship version Auto-Tune 7.

1. Auto-Tune Effect and Standard Pitch Correction Using Auto-Tune EFX 2
2. Tour of Auto-Tune Live
3. Tour of Auto-Tune 7's Automatic Mode
4. Tour of Auto-Tune 7's Graphical Mode
5. Standard (Transparent) Pitch Correction in Auto-Tune 7's Automatic Mode
6. Using Auto-Tune 7's Automatic Mode and Graphical Mode Together
7. Gentle Pitch Correction Using Auto-Tune Graphical Mode's Curve Objects
8. Mixing Effect and Transparent Correction Using Graphical Mode's Line Objects and Note Objects
9. Auto-Tune Effect and Melody Creation Using Auto-Tune 7's Graphical Mode
10. MIDI and the Auto-Tune Effect in Auto-Tune Live

INDEX

32-bit, 9–10
440 Hertz, 25, 40, 96, 102
64-bit, 9, 10, 75

A

Ableton Live, 12
Adjust Vibrato, 56, 66–67, 83–84
Adobe Audition, 12
Aguilera, Christina, 2
All/Tie, 39
Alto/Tenor Voice (Input Type), 23–24
American Idol, 1
Amplitude Amount (Create Vibrato), 31, 78
Antares Audio Technologies, 4, 10
Antares AVP, 5
Apple, 9–10, 12–13
Arrow tool, 47–50, 54, 57, 64–65, 68, 96–97
AU, 6, 8–10, 12–13, 75
Audio Units, 12
Automatic mode (Auto Mode), 23–31, 34,
    36, 39–41, 44, 48, 50, 53–54, 56–58,
    66–67, 71–74, 76, 78–79, 81–83, 87–91,
    93–94, 96, 98–99
Auto-Motion, 6
auto-run settings, 13
Auto Scroll, 38, 72, 96
Auto-Tune, 7, 5, 8–10, 14, 17, 21, 39, 75–76,
    78, 93
Auto-Tune effect, 1, 3, 6, 17, 20, 23, 31, 45,
    49, 61, 63–64, 67, 69. 71, 77, 79–80, 88,
    93–96, 98
Auto-Tune EFX, 1, 93
Auto-Tune EFX, 2, 6, 21, 93
Auto-Tune Evo, 7–8
Auto-Tune Live, 5–6, 9, 21, 23, 75–78
"Auto-Tune the News," 3, 59, 94
Avid/Digidesign, 12

B

Bass Instrument (Instrument Type), 23–24,
    102
"Bed Intruder Song," 3
Black Eyed Peas, 1, 3
Blue Curve Correction objects (Blue Target
    Pitch Contour objects) (Blue Curves),
    42–44, 49, 54–56, 60, 72–73
Buffer Size, 16, 21, 35
Bypass All, 27

C

Cakewalk Sonar, 12
CC, 76–77
Cher, 1–3, 36, 80, 94, 98
Choosy, 24
Chromatic, 24–25, 27, 38, 44, 53, 61, 69
Clear All, 50, 60, 72
Clear All (Time Control), 107, 110
Clock Position, 35, 38
Clock section, 34–35, 66
clock Source, 34
continuous controller, 6, 76–77
correction mode, 20, 23
Create Notes From MIDI, 99
Create Vibrato section, 30–31, 57, 72, 81–82
Cubase, 4, 12, 34, 87
Cursor Time Position display, 51
Curve objects, 36, 40, 44, 45, 47–49, 54, 60,
    69–71, 102–103
Curve tool, 44, 47, 57–59, 67, 85

D

Data Error indicator, 113
Data File Management button, 17
Data File Management dialog, 17–18, 105
DAW, 4–5, 8–14, 16, 20–21, 24–25, 28,
    34–35, 37–38, 40–41, 47, 50–51, 56, 62,
    64, 66, 76–78, 81–82, 87–91, 95–96, 99,
    113
Default Retune Speed, 17, 36, 54, 70, 73, 96
defrag, 13
Detected Pitch display, 41, 50–51
Digital Performer, 12–13
Dion, Celine, 2
"Double Rainbow Song," 3
Drawing Curves, 56–57

E

Edit Scale display, 24–27, 30, 89–90, 94, 96
Effect Type switch, 6
Enable (button), 39, 106–108
Envelope Graph display, 37–39, 48, 106–
    108, 110, 112

F

Fender, 1, 79
Focusrite, 14
Formant Amount, 31, 78, 81–82

Formant button, 25–26, 54, 63, 67
fragmentation, 13

G

GarageBand, 12
Get Info (Apple Command), 10
Graphical mode, 8, 16–17, 19–24, 26, 29–30,
    33–50, 53–54, 56, 58, 60–61, 66–67,
    69–73, 75, 80–81, 83–85, 91, 93, 95–96,
    99, 101–103, 105–107
Graphical mode edit buttons, 49
Green, Al, 1
Green Output Pitch Curves (Green Curves),
    42–44, 60, 63, 66–67, 72, 83–85
Gregory Brothers, 3, 59

H

Hand tool, 48
Host (clock Source), 34–35
"How Soon Is Now," 79
humanization, 8, 58
Humanize, 28–29, 74, 78

I

I-Beam tool, 45–46, 48, 50, 54, 64, 69–70,
    73, 109
iLok System, 11
iLok USB key, 11
Import Auto button, 44, 53–56, 72–73
Input Type, 23–24, 40, 102
Instrument (Input Type), 24, 102
Internal (clock Source), 35

J

Jackson, Randy, 1
Joplin, Janis, 1

K

Key, 21, 24, 26, 40, 44, 53, 61, 69, 72–73, 78,
    87–88, 92, 94–95, 98, 103
Key Bindings, 17
Keyboard Edit, 27, 96
Keyboard Mode, 27
King, B. B., 4

L

Latch Mode, 28
Learn Scale From MIDI, 31, 87–88, 90, 98
Line Correction object (Line object), 36, 45,
    49, 55, 60–68, 70–71
Line tool, 45, 47, 60–61, 63–64, 66

Link Ray, 79
Logic Pro, 10, 12
Low Male (Input Type), 24

M

Macintosh (Mac), 4, 9, 12–13, 48, 65–66, 97
Magnifying Glass tool, 47–48
Make Curve button, 44–45, 54–56, 69, 83
Make Notes button, 40, 44–46, 54, 69–70, 98
MIDI, 6, 8, 23, 31, 44–45, 69, 76–78, 87–92,
    94, 98–99
MIDI pan, 77
MIDI volume, 77
Momentary mode, 28
monophonic, 3–4, 25, 79, 91, 99, 101, 103
MOTU, 12–13
Mountain Lion, 10
Move Point tool, 107–12
Move Region tool, 107, 110–112
MusicXML, 6

N

Natural Vibrato (knob), 28–30, 72, 74,
    80–83
Nicks, Stevie, 79
Note Correction objects (Note objects), 36,
    38, 40, 45–49, 55, 68–71, 80, 91, 95–99
Note lanes, 37–38
Nudge buttons, 46–47, 65
Nuendo, 12, 34

O

Object Pitch display, 50, 92
Octave All, 31, 89–90
Octave As Played, 31, 89–90
OMNI mode, 76–77
Onset Delay (Create Vibrato), 31, 72, 78,
    81–82
Onset Rate (Create Vibrato), 31, 72, 81–82
operating system, 13
Options, 16–17, 35–36, 44, 76–77, 94, 96,
    107
OS X, 9–10, 13
Output Pitch display, 50

P

Pitch Amount (Create Vibrato), 31, 78
pitch analyzer, 50
pitch axis, 37–38
Pitch Change Amount Indicator (Pitch
    Change Amount Meter), 25–26, 41

Pitch Correction Control Section, 28

pitch correction objects, 21, 37, 55, 85, 94, 112

Pitch Graph display, 34, 37–42, 44–50, 54, 57, 60, 64, 67, 69, 70, 72–73, 81, 83, 91–92, 96–98, 106–108, 111–112

Pitch Reference Lines (note lines), 37–38, 40–42, 47–48, 63

Presley, Elvis, 1

Presonus, 14

Program Files (x86), 10

Pro Tools, 1–4, 12–13, 15, 34

Q

QWERTY, 17, 40, 54, 66

R

Rate (Create Vibrato), 30, 78, 81–82

real time pitch correction, 20–21

Red Curves, 41–42, 44, 50, 54–55, 57, 60, 63, 69, 72, 96, 98

Red Input Pitch Contour Data (Red Input Pitch Contour Curves) (Red Curves), 41–45, 50, 54–55, 57, 60, 63 66, 69–70, 72, 84, 91, 96, 98

Redo, 47, 55, 62, 64

Redo (Time Control), 107

reference pitch, 25, 40, 66, 96, 102

Relaxed, 24, 42

Remove All, 27

Retune Speed, 28–29, 36, 48–50, 53–56, 62–64, 66–68, 70–71, 73, 77–78, 80–82, 84–85, 91, 93–96, 102–103

Retune Speed (per Object), 44, 48, 64, 66–67, 96, 102

RTAS (Real Time AudioSuite), 6, 8–9, 12–13, 75

"Rumble," 79

S

Scale (parameter), 21, 22, 24–29, 40, 44–45, 47, 53, 61, 69, 71–73, 78, 92, 94–95, 98, 103

Scale Detune, 25–26, 40, 73

Scissors tool, 49, 54, 68, 96–97

Set Major, 26–27

Set Minor, 26–27

Shape (Create Vibrato), 30, 72, 78, 81–82

Show Lanes, 38, 45, 60, 69, 96

signal path, 15, 21

signal processors, 15

Sinatra, Frank, 1

Smiths, The, 79

Snap to Note, 46–47, 60, 63, 65, 69

Sony Vegas, 12

Soprano (Input Type), 23–24

"Star Spangled Banner, The," 79

Steinberg, 4, 12

Studio 1, 12

T

Target notes, 8, 25–27, 31, 78, 80, 87–90, 94, 98

Target Notes Via MIDI, 31, 78, 87, 90, 98

Targeting Ignores Vibrato, 29, 72, 74, 83

TASCAM's TA-1VP, 5, 21

Taylor, Mark, 2

TDM (Time Division Multiplex), 8–9, 12–13, 15, 75

Throat Length, 25–26, 40, 67, 78, 103

Throat Length Adjust, 56, 66–67

Time Control section, 106–108, 110

Time Display, 38, 51

time tools, 47, 107–108, 112

T-Pain, 1, 3, 36, 80, 94, 98

Track Pitch (button), 40, 72, 113

Track Pitch + Time (button), 39–40, 106, 108

Tracking (parameter), 21, 23–24, 40, 42, 102

Transpose (parameter), 25, 40, 94–95

tremolo, 31, 79, 81

U

Undo, 17, 46, 49, 55, 60, 61–64,

Undo (Time Control), 107, 110, 112

V

Variation (Create Vibrato), 31, 78, 81–82

vibrato, 21, 23, 28–31, 44, 46, 50, 54–55, 57–58, 66–68, 70, 79–85, 102

Virtual Keyboard, 27–28, 89, 96

Virtual Keyboard color codes, 28

VST (Virtual Studio Technology), 6, 8–10, 12, 75

W

Wavelab, 12

West, Kanye, 3, 94

whammy bar, 79

Windows, 4, 9–10, 12–14, 48, 65–66, 97

quick PRO

guides *series*

Producing Music with Ableton Live
by Jake Perrine
Softcover w/DVD-ROM •
978-1-4584-0036-9 • $16.99

Sound Design, Mixing, and Mastering with Ableton Live
by Jake Perrine
Softcover w/DVD-ROM •
978-1-4584-0037-6 • $16.99

Mixing and Mastering with Cubase
by Matthew Loel T. Hepworth
Softcover w/DVD-ROM •
978-1-4584-1367-3 • $16.99

The Power in Cubase: Tracking Audio, MIDI, and Virtual Instruments
by Matthew Loel T. Hepworth
Softcover w/DVD-ROM •
978-1-4584-1366-6 • $16.99

The Power in Digital Performer
by David E. Roberts
Softcover w/DVD-ROM •
978-1-4768-1514-5 • $16.99

Logic Pro for Recording Engineers and Producers
by Dot Bustelo
Softcover w/DVD-ROM •
978-1-4584-1420-5 • $16.99

The Power in Logic Pro: Songwriting, Composing, Remixing, and Making Beats
by Dot Bustelo
Softcover w/DVD-ROM •
978-1-4584-1419-9 • $16.99

Mixing and Mastering with Pro Tools
by Glenn Lorbecki
Softcover w/DVD-ROM •
978-1-4584-0033-8 •$16.99

Tracking Instruments and Vocals with Pro Tools
by Glenn Lorbecki
Softcover w/DVD-ROM •
978-1-4584-0034-5 •$16.99

The Power in Reason
by Andrew Eisele
Softcover w/DVD-ROM •
978-1-4584-0228-8 • $16.99

Sound Design and Mixing in Reason
by Andrew Eisele
Softcover w/DVD-ROM •
978-1-4584-0229-5 • $16.99

Studio One for Engineers and Producers
by William Edstrom, Jr.
Softcover w/DVD-ROM •
978-1-4768-0602-0 • $16.99

HAL•LEONARD®
quickproguides.halleonardbooks.com
Prices, contents, and availability subject to change without notice.

0113